THE LIBRARY
OF
AMERICAN BIOGRAPHY
CONDUCTED BY
Jared Sparks.

P. Henry

BOSTON,
CHARLES C. LITTLE AND JAMES BROWN.

THE LIFE

OF

PATRICK HENRY

Alexander H. Everett, LL.D.

HERITAGE BOOKS
2025

HERITAGE BOOKS
AN IMPRINT OF HERITAGE BOOKS, INC.

Books, CDs, and more—Worldwide

For our listing of thousands of titles see our website
at
www.HeritageBooks.com

A Facsimile Reprint
Published 2025 by
HERITAGE BOOKS, INC.
Publishing Division
5810 Ruatan Street
Berwyn Heights, MD 20740

Entered according to act of Congress in the year 1844, by
Charles C. Little and James Brown,
In the Clerk's office of the District Court of the District of Massachusetts

Boston:
Charles C. Little and James Brown.
1844.

— Publisher's Notice —
In reprints such as this, it is often not possible to remove
blemishes from the original. We feel the contents of this
book warrant its reissue despite these blemishes and
hope you will agree and read it with pleasure.

International Standard Book Number
Paperbound: 978-0-7884-7701-0

LIFE OF PATRICK HENRY.

BY ALEXANDER H. EVERETT.

CHAPTER I.

Birth and Parentage. — Education. — Commences Business as a Merchant. — Fails, and attempts Agriculture. — Second unsuccessful Attempt in Trade. — Marriage. — Admitted to the Bar. 209

CHAPTER II.

The Parsons' Cause. — First remarkable Exhibition of Henry's Eloquence. 227

CHAPTER III.

Elected a Member of the House of Burgesses. — Brings forward his celebrated Resolutions on the Stamp Act. 250

CHAPTER IV.

Repeal of the Stamp Act. — Henry elected to the Continental Congress. — Speech in the Virginia Convention. 275

CHAPTER V.

Military Movements. — Henry appointed Commander-in-Chief of the Virginia Forces. — Resigns his Commission. — Elected the first Governor under the new Constitution. . . . 296

CHAPTER VI.

Administration as Governor. — Returns to private Life. — Reëlected Governor. — Resigns. — Elected to the Assembly. 324

CHAPTER VII.

Virginia Convention for considering the Plan of the Federal Constitution. — Henry opposes its Adoption. 348

CHAPTER VIII.

Retirement of Henry from political and professional Life. — Domestic Occupations. — Death and Character. 376

NOTE.

Virginia Resolutions on the Stamp Act. . . . 391

PATRICK HENRY.

CHAPTER I.

Birth and Parentage. — Education. — Commences Business as a Merchant. — Fails, and attempts Agriculture. — Second unsuccessful Attempt in Trade. — Marriage. — Admitted to the Bar.

PATRICK HENRY is, in more than in one particular, among the most remarkable characters of the revolutionary period of our history. He is declared by Jefferson to have been "the greatest orator that ever lived," and "the person who, beyond all question, gave the first impulse to the movement, which terminated in the revolution." Whatever exaggeration, if any, may be supposed to have crept into these sweeping statements, it is certain that the merits and services which had power to call them forth from such a quarter, must have been of no ordinary kind.

Indeed, the accounts that have been transmitted to us of the actual effects of his eloquence upon the minds of his hearers, though resting apparently on the best authority, seem almost fabulous, and certainly surpass any that we have on record of the results produced by the most distinguished orators of ancient or modern Europe. Something must probably be allowed for the excited imagination of the authors of these accounts; but the necessity for making this allowance proves, of itself, the extent to which Henry possessed what may be regarded as the essence of the highest kind of eloquence, and powers of strongly exciting the imagination of his hearers.

His claim to the honor of having given the first impulse to the revolutionary movement, is a question hardly susceptible of a satisfactory solution, since no event, prior to the battle of Lexington and the declaration of independence, was so decidedly different in character from a variety of others occurring at about the same time, as to merit, in contradistinction from them, the praise of being the first step in the progress of the revolution. It is certain, however, that, in one of the two leading colonies, during the period immediately preceding the revolution, Henry was constantly in advance of the most ardent patriots, and that he suggested and carried into effect, by his immediate personal influence, measures that were opposed as premature and violent by all the other eminent supporters of the cause of liberty. It was the good fortune of Henry to enjoy, during his lifetime, the appropriate reward of his extraordinary merits, and the almost unbounded admiration and respect of his countrymen.

By general acknowledgment, the greatest orator of his day; elevated by his transcendent talents to a sort of supremacy in the deliberative assemblies of which he was occasionally a member, and the courts of justice in which he exercised his profession; clothed, whenever he chose to accept them, with the highest executive functions in the gift of the people; happy in his domestic relations and private circumstances, — his career was one of almost unbroken prosperity. He has also been eminently fortunate in the manner in which the history of his life has been written. While the recollection of his eloquence and the admiration of his character were still fresh in the minds of numerous surviving contemporaries, the task of collecting and recording the expressions of them, which were circulating in conversation, or merely ephemeral notes, was undertaken by one whose kindred eloquence and virtues rendered him on every account the fittest person to do justice to the subject. In the following sketch, I can claim little other merit, than that of condensing, with perhaps some few not very important modifications and additions, the glowing biography of Wirt.

The gifted author is represented, on the same high authority alluded to above, that of Jefferson, as having been at times led by the enthusiasm with which he entered into his subject, to the verge of fiction. Let us also apply to his work the title which the great German poet, Goethe, prefixed to his own autobiography, — *Poetry and Truth*. The narrative carries with it unquestionable evidence of authenticity, as well in the known character of the writer as in the authorities that are cited in support of every important statement, while it is written with so much warmth and elegance, that it possesses, throughout, all the charm of poetry, and perhaps produces, at times, a similar illusion. Although some few passages are a little too highly colored for the eye of good taste, there are few persons of eminence, who, after reading the whole, would not feel the wish which Queen Katharine, in the play, expressed in regard to her attendant, Griffith, that they might find themselves as fond and faithful a chronicler.

The family of Patrick Henry was of Scottish origin. His father, John Henry, was a native of Aberdeen; and he numbered among his family connections some of the distinguished literary men of the day, having been a nephew, in the maternal line, to the historian Robertson, and cousin to David Henry, the brother-in-law to Edward Cave, and his successor in the conduct of the Gentleman's Magazine. John Henry emigrated to Virginia some time before the year 1730. He is said to have enjoyed the friendship and patronage of Dinwiddie, afterwards governor of the colony, who introduced him to the elder Colonel Syme, of Hanover county. In the family of the latter, Henry became domesticated, and, after the death of the colonel, married his widow, and resided on the estate. He appears to have enjoyed much consideration among his fellow-citizens, having been colonel of his regiment, principal surveyor of the county, and, for many years, presiding magistrate of the county court. Some years after his emigration, his brother Patrick, a clergyman of the Church of England, followed him to Virginia, and became, by his influence, minister of St. Paul's parish in Hanover, a place which he filled through life with high distinction. Both the brothers were conspicuous for their loyalty to the king and attachment to the church.

The widow of Colonel Syme, who became, as has been said, the wife of John Henry and the mother of Patrick, was a native of Hanover county, and a daughter of the family of Winston, one of the most respectable in the colony. So far as the eloquence of Patrick Henry may be supposed to have been in any degree hereditary, it seems to have been transmitted to him through the maternal line. His mother is represented as having been remarkable for a fluent and easy elocution, and her brother, Judge Winston, was declared by a contemporary, who knew him well, to have been the greatest orator whom he had ever heard, Patrick Henry alone excepted. When the militia of Virginia were ordered, soon after Braddock's defeat, to the frontiers, the company to which Winston belonged, and of which he was lieutenant, were so much disheartened by the severity of the service, that they were on the point of breaking out into mutiny, when Winston, by a well-timed stump speech, succeeded in restoring order, and inspired them with so much enthusiasm, that they called upon their officers to lead them at once against the enemy.

It appears, from these statements, that the family of Patrick Henry was among the most distinguished in the colony. He was the second of nine children, and was born on the 29th of May, 1736, at the family seat in Hanover county, called Studley. His father removed, not long after, to another seat in the same county, then called Mount Brilliant, and now the Retreat; and it was here that Patrick was educated. The family, though evidently in easy circumstances, does not seem to have been wealthy. The father had opened a grammar school in his own house; and Patrick, after having acquired the elements of learning at an infant school in the neighborhood, was taken home, at ten years of age, to continue his studies. Under his father's tuition, he obtained some little smattering of the Latin language and of mathematics. He had no inclination whatever for book learning. As the discipline of such a school was not likely to be severe, he seems to have indulged, without much restraint, his taste for rural sports and solitary rambles through the neighboring fields and forests. At this period, he showed no sign of the high intellectual qualities for which he was afterwards distinguished. His personal appearance and manners were coarse and awkward, his dress neglected, and his faculties entirely obscured by habitual indolence. In mixed companies, he contributed little or nothing to the conversation, but is said to have listened with attention, and to have been able afterwards to repeat much of what had been said, with intelligent comments on the characters of the speakers. This is the only particular in his youthful habits that has since been recollected, as having indicated in any degree his future superiority.

Finding him wholly indisposed for literary and professional pursuits, his father undertook to establish him in trade; and, after placing him for a year in the counting-room of a neighboring merchant, furnished him and his brother William with a small capital, upon which they commenced business. William, it seems, was still more indolent than his brother; so that the management of the common concern devolved chiefly upon Patrick, who displayed as little aptitude for mercantile affairs as he had previously done for study. The confinement which this employment rendered necessary was irksome to him; and, although he was afterwards remarked for a rather thrifty disposition in his pecuniary affairs, the consequence, probably, of early embarrassments, he exhibited at this time an easiness of temper, and a negligence in making his bargains, which were not favorable to the success of the enterprise. Compelled to relinquish his habitual sports, he resorted, as a substitute for them, to music, and learned to play upon the violin and flute.

He also began, for the first time, to show some taste for reading; and exhibited, with increasing distinctness, the talent for nice observation of character which he had shown in his childhood. He encouraged his customers, when they met in his shop, to discuss questions which he suggested for their consideration; and, without taking much part himself in the debate, derived his principal amusement from comparing their habits of thought and action, as developed in the course of their respective remarks. At other times, he entertained them by narratives gathered from his miscellaneous reading, or framed by himself for the purpose. In these intellectual exercises we begin to perceive the first dawning of the brilliant talents by which, in after years, he so often entranced his audience. They seem, however, to have had no very favorable effect upon the success of his enterprise, which, after the experiment of a year, proved a failure. William retired at once from the concern, while Patrick was employed for two or three years afterwards in bringing it to a close as well as he could. In the mean time, at the age of eighteen, he had married Miss Shelton, the daughter of a neighboring farmer, of excellent character, but of narrow worldly fortune.

Unsuccessful alike in letters and in trade, the future orator, or more probably his friends, now directed his attention to agriculture. By the joint aid of the two families the newly-married couple were placed upon a small farm, from which, with the aid of one or two slaves, with whom they were also provided, they were to draw, by the sweat of their brows, the means of subsistence. But the indolent habits, and aversion to systematic labor of any kind, which had occasioned the failure of his former attempts to effect a permanent establishment, were equally fatal to this. After an experiment of two years, he abandoned the plan, sold his property at a loss for cash, invested the proceeds in merchandise, and once more tempted fortune in the lottery of trade. In resuming his business as a merchant, he also resumed his former habits of conducting it. He employed, as before, a large portion of his time in conversation with his customers, or in music and light reading; and he frequently closed his warehouse for the purpose of pursuing his favorite recreations in the open air. Thus conducted, it is not very singular that, after another two years' trial, the second experiment in trade ended, like the former, in bankruptcy.

The position of Henry, in a worldly view, was now sufficiently embarrassing. He had lost all his little property, and had no capacity for supporting his family by any of the usual professions. His connections had done all they could for him. A feebler mind would have probably sunk under this complication of difficulties. Henry, far from being in any degree discouraged, was roused by it to the exertions which alone were necessary to the development of his splendid powers. Possessed, as he was at this time, by an unconquerable passion for amusement, probably nothing but absolute necessity of the most urgent kind could have furnished the spur that was wanting to his success; so that he might afterwards have said, with great propriety, in the words of an ancient, "I should have been ruined, if I had not been ruined." His biographers do not, however, appear to have appreciated his character with perfect correctness, when they attribute these repeated failures, in his attempts in business of different kinds, to mere indolence. His mind was not deficient in a principle of activity, but at this period it took exclusively the direction of amusement. The indispensable necessity of pursuing, with steady industry, the substantial objects of life, had not yet been brought home to him, and he yielded without resistance to the promptings of his naturally exuberant animal spirits. Even at the lowest ebb of his worldly fortunes, his disposition for sport and pleasantry remained unimpaired. Mr. Jefferson saw him for the first time at this period, and afterwards gave, in a letter to Mr. Wirt, the following account of his appearance and manners. Henry was then twenty-four years of age.

"My acquaintance with Mr. Henry commenced in the year 1759–60. On my way to the college, I passed the Christmas holydays at

Colonel Dandridge's, in Hanover, to whom Mr. Henry was a near neighbor. During the festivity of the season, I met him in society every day, and we became well acquainted, although I was much his junior, being then in my seventeenth year, and he a married man. His manners had something of coarseness in them; his passion was music, dancing, and pleasantry. He excelled in the last, and it attached every one to him. You ask some account of his mind and information at this period; but you will recollect that we were almost continually engaged in the usual revelries of the season. The occasion, perhaps, as much as his idle disposition, prevented his engaging in any conversation, which might give the measure of his mind or information. Opportunity was not, indeed, wholly wanting, because Mr. John Campbell was there, who had married Mrs. Spotswood, the sister of Colonel Dandridge. He was a man of science, and often introduced conversation on scientific subjects. Mr. Henry had, a little before, broken up his store, or rather it had broken him up; but his misfortunes were not to be traced either in his countenance or conduct."

But though the absorbing passion for pleasure, which at this time formed the distinguishing characteristic of Henry's mind, had been fatal to his success in the various employments which he had hitherto attempted, it had not entirely deprived him of proper intellectual culture. During his first experiment in trade, he had devoted, as has been said, a part of his leisure to light reading. In the course of the second, which was of somewhat longer duration, he extended his studies to subjects of a more serious character, and made himself familiar with geography and history, particularly the documentary and political history of Virginia. *Multum, non multa,* (much, but not a great many books,) is the well-known rule for judicious and profitable reading.

This rule was enforced upon Henry by the circumstances of the times and country in which he lived. Cheap literature was not yet in fashion, and in settlements so remote from the central points of civilization as the interior of Virginia then was, the supply of even standard works was not very abundant. A person who had acquired a taste for reading could only gratify it by repeated perusals of a few writers. The historians of Greece and Rome, whom he read in English translations, were his favorite study. Livy, in particular, was a sort of manual with him; and he subsequently informed a friend, that, in the earlier part of his life, he made it a rule to read the whole of this charming writer at least as often as once in every year. The

Virginian Demosthenes was imitating, perhaps
without knowing it, the example of his great
prototype, who is said to have copied the whole
of Thucydides eight times with his own hand.
The remarkable and significant fact just alluded
to shows the vigor with which Henry's naturally
elevated mind, though incapable of binding itself
down to the uncongenial tasks, which had thus
far been presented to it, soared above the sphere
of its habitual pursuits and pleasures in search
of intellectual nutriment suited to its character.

How infinitely preferable was this course of
reading, whether considered in its effect on the
judgment, the feelings, or the taste, to the confused mass of magazines, reviews, and novels,
that occupy the hours of students of the
present day! In the constant use of this noble
manual we may, no doubt, trace, in no slight
degree, the energy of purpose, the high tone of
moral sentiment, the sound practical wisdom,
in short, the Roman cast of character, using the
phrase in the very best sense, which marked,
throughout, the course of Henry, and which, but
for the fact just mentioned, would have been
unexplained by any known circumstances in his
early pursuits and studies. With such training,
however irregularly obtained, and with the
splendid capacities, which were yet to be developed, it only remained for Henry to place

himself in a situation where his talents would be brought into exercise, in order to assume at once the eminent position to which they entitled him. The moment was, however, critical; another mistake in the choice of a profession, like those which he had already made, and ending in a continuation of his former ill success, would have condemned him for life to hopeless dependence and utter insignificance. On the contrary, he was still young enough to reclaim, by a vigorous application of his powers to the uses for which they were intended, the time that he had lost, and to enter, with still unclouded prospects of success, on the business of life.

Everything depended on the course, which he was now to take; and his decision proved to be a most fortunate one for himself and his country. Baffled in his efforts to provide for his family in any of the less conspicuous occupations, he resolved to grasp at the highest and most difficult of all, the practice of law. It may be doubted, however, whether his views, in adopting the legal profession, went beyond the acquisition of a moderate subsistence. He was still unconscious of the extent of his abilities, and may, perhaps, have been determined on selecting another employment, by the fact, that he could attempt the bar without the necessity of a moneyed capital, rather than by any anticipation of the eminence which he afterwards acquired. His situation rendered it, of course, important to contract as much as possible the time of preparation.

Judge Tyler, the father of the present president of the United States, was informed by Henry himself, that he devoted one month only to this purpose, during which he read only Coke upon Littleton, and the Virginia statutes. Mr. Jefferson, who was in the college at Williamsburg when Henry came there to obtain his license, was told by himself, that he had studied only six weeks. Other accounts fix the time at six, eight, and nine months; but these variations are of little importance. It was not unnatural, that, under these circumstances, he should have found some difficulty in obtaining the necessary license from the board of examiners, which appears to have consisted of John and Peyton Randolph, Judge Wythe, and Robert C. Nicholas, all of them persons of superior talent and the highest eminence in the profession. According to the account of Mr. Jefferson, who was on the spot at the time, and partially acquainted with the circumstances, though he may not have remembered them so accurately as Henry himself, the two Randolphs, who were persons of great facility of temper, first consented to sign the license, though with great reluctance. Wythe positively refused, and Nicholas at first declined, but finally, after great importunity and promises of future reading, gave his name, which completed the necessary number.

In the account given by Judge Tyler of a conversation which he had with Henry himself on the same subject, he is represented as having said, that, after obtaining the signatures of two of the examiners, he presented himself to John Randolph, afterwards attorney-general of the colony, a profound lawyer and a finished gentleman. Finding how little he had read, and not being favorably impressed with his appearance and manner, Randolph at first refused to examine Henry, but at length, on being told that he had already obtained two signatures, began to interrogate him, though with evident reluctance. The replies made by Henry satisfied him at once that he was no common man. He then entered upon an examination, which lasted several hours, embracing not only the local and colonial law, but the whole field of jurisprudence, in its widest extent, including the law of nations and general history. In the course of the examination, in order to test the logical ability of the candidate, Randolph disputed some of his positions, and drew him into a discussion, at the close of which he admitted that Henry had the best of the argument. He finally gave his signature, with the flattering remark, that he would never be deceived by appearances again; and that, if Henry's industry should be at all proportioned to his genius, he would become very shortly an ornament to his profession.

Such were the auspices under which Patrick Henry was admitted to the bar. Ignorant, as he was, not only of law as a science, and of the most familiar forms of its practical administration, incapable, as is said, of drawing a declaration or making a motion in court, it is not very wonderful that he obtained at first but little employment. His uncle, Judge Winston, states, that, during the first four years after he received his license, he remained entirely undistinguished. His circumstances were extremely narrow, and he appears to have resided the greater part of the time with his father-in-law, Mr. Shelton, who then kept a tavern at Hanover court-house. When Shelton was absent from home, Henry officiated in his stead, and probably lent him at other times such aid as was necessary. This fact accounts for the statement, which has sometimes been made, and which does not seem to be very far from the truth, that he was, at one period in his early life, a bar-keeper at a tavern.

The rumor, so far as it is well founded, adds another to the numerous occupations, through which the brilliant orator was compelled to make his way to distinction. At length the clouds, that had so long hovered over his prospects, cleared away. The celebrated *Parsons' Cause*, as it is still called in Virginia, afforded him the opportunity, which alone was wanting, to establish his powers, and placed him at once at the head of the profession.

CHAPTER II.

The Parsons' Cause. — First remarkable Exhibition of Henry's Eloquence.

The account of the Parsons' Cause is one of those passages in the life of Henry, in which poetry appears to be in some degree mingled with truth; nor is it easy, with the information now before us, to say, with entire certainty, what parts of the narrative appertain respectively to one or the other of these departments. The particulars of the affair are briefly as follows.

The Parsons' Cause was an action brought by the Rev. James Maury, in the county court of Hanover county, against the collector of taxes for that county and his sureties, for the recovery of damages for the non-payment of a certain quantity of tobacco, alleged to be due to him on account of his salary. The claim was founded in a statute of the colony, originally passed in the year 1696, and reënacted, with amendments, in the year 1748, which fixed the annual stipend of a parish minister at sixteen thousand pounds of tobacco, and authorized him to demand payment in the article itself. He was, of course, at liberty to receive it in any other way that might suit his convenience. The common market price of tobacco had, for a long time, remained stationary at two pence the pound, or sixteen shillings and eight pence the hundred, and the clergy were in the habit of commuting the delivery of the article in kind for a money payment calculated on this basis.

In the year 1755, the crop of tobacco having fallen short, the price rose to fifty or sixty shillings the hundred. In order to relieve the planters from the effect of this accidental change in the value of the article, the legislature passed an act authorizing them, for the present year, to pay in money such of these debts as might be due in tobacco, at the rate of sixteen shillings and eight pence the hundred. The act was to continue in force for ten months, and went into effect immediately, not having contained the clause which was usually inserted in the acts of the colonial legislature, suspending their operation until they should receive the royal assent. No opposition was made by the clergy to the execution of this law, which was regularly carried into effect during the period for which it was enacted.

Three years afterwards, in the year 1758, in consequence of the probability of the occurrence of another short crop, the law of 1755 was reënacted, and, as before, without the clause requiring the royal assent. The clergy now took alarm, and the measure was attacked in a vigorous pamphlet, entitled *The Two-penny Act*, published by the Rev. John Camm, rector of York-Hampton parish, and Episcopalian commissary for the colony. He was answered in two pamphlets, one written by Colonel Richard Bland, and the other by Colonel Landon Carter, in which the commissary was treated without much ceremony. He replied in a still more pointed pamphlet, entitled *The Colonels Dismounted*. The colonels rejoined, and a war of pamphlets followed, which created a great excitement throughout the colony. The popular sentiment appears to have been adverse to the pretensions of the clergy, and at length became so strong, that the printers within the colony refused to publish for them, so that Mr. Camm was finally compelled to resort to Maryland for a publisher.

The pamphlets, which were elicited by this

controversy, are still extant, and Mr. Wirt remarks, that "It seems impossible to deny, at this day, that the clergy had much the best of the argument." This, however, seems to be a merely technical view of the subject, founded on the idea, that the colonial laws were not valid without the royal assent, and that the clergy had, of course, retained, throughout the whole affair, all the rights, that were vested in them by the act of 1748. Such, probably, was the correct construction of the law; but it seems to be clear, that the equity of the affair was on the other side, and that, so far as the argument turned upon any other topic than that of strict legal right, the planters were able to make out a very strong case. The act of 1748 was a liberal and beneficial statute, intended to secure the clergy against the effect of fluctuations in the value of money; and it was hardly fair or honorable in the clergy to take advantage of this act of liberality in the planters, to extort from them, in a time of scarcity, triple the amount of the usual stipend. If the rise in the price of tobacco had been the effect of a depreciation in the value of money, and had extended to all other articles, the equity would have been with the clergy, because they could not have obtained the real value of their usual stipend without receiving it in kind.

But as the rise took place in the article of tobacco only, being the effect of a short crop, while the value of money remained the same, the clergy, by commuting the payment in tobacco for a money payment at the former price, would have received the full amount of their usual salary, and this was all that they could fairly claim. Mr. Wirt remarks, that they could not help observing the benefits resulting from the act to the rich planters, who received fifty or sixty shillings the hundred for their tobacco, while they were paying their tobacco debts at the rate of sixteen shillings and eight pence. He does not seem to have recollected, that the rise in the price of tobacco was the effect of a reduction in the quantity. If the planter, by selling a crop of only a third of the ordinary amount, for three times the usual price, was able to avoid the injurious effect of a short crop, he was still in no better condition than he would have been if the rise had not occurred; and if he paid his tobacco debts in kind at the existing high prices, he sustained an actual loss equal to two thirds of the amount due. It was not fair, as has been remarked, for the clergy to extort this difference under pretence of a law, which the planters had passed for the relief and benefit of the order. If, therefore, the law was with the clergy, the equity was clearly with the planters.

The legal objection to the act of 1748 was also one of the narrowest kind, and was, in reality, scarcely tenable.

Admitting, as a general rule, that the acts of a colonial legislature were not valid without the royal assent, it could not well be denied, that a legislature, situated at such an immense distance from the mother country, must be supposed to possess some discretionary power to proceed without direct authority from home in a case of real necessity, and this was obviously one of that kind. The state of the crop could not be ascertained much in advance of the time when it would be brought to market; and, in order to meet the emergency, the law must be enacted, and carried into effect, before, in that day of protracted voyages and slow communications, there would be time to submit it to the eye of majesty. If substantial justice required the adoption of such a measure, and it was really impossible, under the circumstances, to have the royal assent, the act might well have been regarded, even without such assent, as technically valid; more especially as the mutual prerogatives of the local and imperial governments were far from being accurately settled. At all events, the right, taking into view both law and equity, was by no means so clearly on the side of the clergy as Mr. Wirt represents it; and it is not at all surprising that the champions of the planters, arguing the case, as they probably did, chiefly on grounds of common sense and substantial justice, were able to make a strong impression upon the minds of the people.

The affair was brought before the king in council; and that body, sustaining naturally enough the construction of the law, and favorable to the royal prerogative, declared the act of 1758 null and void, for want of the royal assent. Finding themselves supported in their pretensions by this high authority, the clergy undertook to enforce them by legal process, and commenced a number of suits for the recovery of their salaries in tobacco, of which that instituted by Maury was one. Another of the same kind was commenced in the same county by the Rev. Patrick Henry, who has already been mentioned as the orator's uncle. The fact that Henry was not employed by his uncle in this interesting cause is a strong proof that little was yet expected, even by those who knew him best, and felt the deepest interest in his welfare, from his future efforts in his new profession.

The plaintiff, in this case of Maury, as I have remarked before, founded his claim in the statute of 1748. The defendant pleaded specially that of 1758; and to this plea the plaintiff demurred;

or, in other words, replied that this act could not operate, in law, to set aside the plaintiff's claim; first, because it had not received the royal assent, and, secondly, because it had been declared null and void by the king in council. The legal question was argued at the November term of the year 1763, by Mr. Lyons for the plaintiff, and Mr. John Lewis for the defendants, when the court, "very much," says Mr. Wirt, "to the credit of their candor and firmness, breasted the popular current by sustaining the demurrer." The clergy, having obtained a decision of the court in their favor, on the only objection that had been raised by the planters, naturally considered their cause as gained. It only remained for a jury to give the damages; but this was regarded as a merely formal proceeding, because the amount was supposed to be settled by the statute of 1748. The action was continued for this purpose; but the counsel for the defendants, Mr. Lewis, viewing the only point of importance as settled, and his services as no longer necessary, retired from the case. It was at this stage in the progress of the affair, and in consequence of the retirement of Mr. Lewis, that Patrick Henry was retained by the defendants. Probably the case was now supposed to have been brought within so narrow a compass, that it might be safely intrusted to a junior member of the bar, hitherto unknown to the public.

Whatever may have been the views of the defendants in retaining him, Henry, on being applied to, consented to take charge of the affair, and to argue the question of damages before the jury. The case came on for trial on the 1st of December, 1763, before the county court, in which the father of Henry sat as presiding magistrate. The position of the young barrister was, in fact, a rather singular one. He was to speak, for the first time in open court, before his own father, as presiding magistrate, in a case in which the court had already given a deliberate opinion in favor of the other party, and in which his uncle was interested against him.

The excitement on the subject was so great throughout the colony, that, even at this late period in the proceedings, a large audience attended, not only from Hanover, but from the neighboring counties. The clergy, in particular, appeared in great force, and among them came the orator's uncle. On seeing him approach, Henry walked up to him, in company with Colonel Meredith, and expressed his regret at seeing his uncle there. "Why so?" inquired the uncle. "Because," replied Henry, "I fear that, as I have never yet spoken in public, I shall be too much overawed by your presence to do justice to my clients. Besides," he added, "I shall be under the necessity of saying some *hard things* of the clergy, which it may be unpleasant to you to hear." His uncle now censured him for having undertaken the case on the side of the planters, which Henry excused by saying that he had had no offer from the clergy; and that, independently of this, his own heart and judgment were on the side of the people. He then requested his uncle to leave the ground. "Why, Patrick," said the old gentleman, with a good-natured smile, "as to *your* saying hard things of the clergy, I advise you to be cautious, as you will be more likely to injure your own cause than theirs. As to my leaving the ground, I fear, my boy, that, with such a case to defend, my presence will do you but little harm or good. Since, however, you seem to think otherwise, and desire it of me so earnestly, you shall be gratified." He then entered his carriage again, and returned home.

This little anecdote, which I have given nearly in the words of Mr. Wirt, is equally creditable to both parties, and affords a pleasing proof of the mutual good feeling, which, under somewhat trying circumstances, was maintained among the different members of the family. It is impossible to do full justice to the scene that followed, without quoting the description of it in the language of the eloquent biographer.

"Soon after the opening of the court, the cause was called. It stood on a writ of inquiry of damages, no plea having been entered by the defendants since the judgment on the demurrer. The array before Mr. Henry's eyes was now most fearful. On the bench sat more than twenty clergymen, the most learned men in the colony, and the most capable, as well as the severest critics before whom it was possible for him to have made his *début*. The court-house was crowded with an overwhelming multitude, and surrounded with an immense and anxious throng, who, not finding room to enter, were endeavoring to listen without in the deepest attention. But there was something still more awfully disconcerting than all this; for in the chair of the presiding magistrate sat no other person than his own father. Mr. Lyons opened the case very briefly. In the way of argument he did nothing more than explain to the jury that the decision upon the demurrer had put the act of 1758 entirely out of the way, and left the law of 1748 as the only standard of damages. He then concluded with a highly-wrought eulogium on the benevolence of the clergy.

"And now came on the first trial of Patrick Henry's strength. No one had ever heard him speak, and curiosity was on tiptoe. He rose very awkwardly, and faltered much in his exordium. The people hung their heads at so unpromising a commencement; the clergy were observed to exchange sly looks with each other, and his father is described as having almost sunk with confusion from his seat. But these feelings were of short duration, and soon gave place to others of a different character. For now were those wonderful faculties which he possessed, for the first time, developed, and now was first witnessed that mysterious and almost supernatural transformation of appearance, which the fire of his own eloquence never failed to work in him. For, as his mind rolled along, and began to glow from its own action, all the *exuriæ* of the clown seemed to shed themselves spontaneously. His attitude, by degrees, became erect and lofty. The spirit of his genius awakened all his features. His countenance shone with a nobleness and grandeur which it had never before exhibited. There was a lightning in his eyes that seemed to rive the spectator. His action became graceful, bold, and commanding; and in the tones of his voice, but more especially in his emphasis, there was a peculiar charm, a magic, of which any one, who ever heard him, will speak as soon as he is named, but of which no one can give any ade-

quate description. They can only say that it
struck upon the ear and upon the heart, *in a
manner which language cannot tell.* Add to all
these his wonder-working fancy, and the peculiar
phraseology in which he clothed his images; for
he painted to the heart with a force that almost
petrified it. In the language of those who heard
him on this occasion, 'he made their blood run
cold, and their hair to rise on end.'

"It will not be difficult for any one, who ever
heard this most extraordinary man, to believe
the whole account of this transaction, which is
given by his surviving hearers; and from their
account the court-house at Hanover must have
exhibited, on this occasion, a scene as picturesque
as has ever been witnessed in real life. They
say that the people, whose countenances had
fallen as he arose, had heard but a very few
sentences before they began to look up; then to
look at each other with surprise, as if doubting
the evidence of their own senses; then, attracted by some strong gesture, struck by some
majestic attitude, fascinated by the spell of his
eye, the charm of his emphasis, and the varied
and commanding expression of his countenance,
they could look away no more. In less than
twenty minutes, they might be seen in every part
of the house, on every bench, in every window,
stooping forward from their stands, in death-like

silence; their features fixed in amazement and awe; all their senses listening and riveted upon the speaker, as if to catch the last strain of some heavenly visitant. The mockery of the clergy was soon turned into alarm: their triumph into confusion and despair; and, at one burst of his rapid and overwhelming invective, *they fled from the bench in precipitation and terror.* As for the father, such was his surprise, such his amazement, such his rapture, that, forgetting where he was, and the character which he was filling, tears of ecstasy streamed down his cheeks, without the power or inclination to repress them.

"The jury seem to have been so completely bewildered that they lost sight not only of the act of 1748, but of that of 1758 also; for, thoughtless even of the admitted right of the plaintiff, they had scarcely left the bar, when they returned with a verdict of *one penny damages.* A motion was made for a new trial; but the court, too, had now lost the equipoise of their judgment, and overruled the motion by a unanimous vote. The verdict and judgment overruling the motion were followed by redoubled acclamations from within and without the house. The people, who had with difficulty kept their hands off their champion, from the moment of his closing his harangue, no sooner saw the fate of the cause finally sealed, than they seized him at the bar, and, in spite of his own exertions and the continued cry of 'Order,' from the sheriff and the court, they bore him out of the court-house, and, raising him on their shoulders, carried him about the yard in a kind of electioneering triumph."

His father is represented as having been so much overwhelmed as to lose, for the time, the power of expressing his feelings. A few days after, in conversation with his brother-in-law, Judge Winston, he alluded to the scene in the following simple terms, which contrast rather singularly with the gorgeous phraseology of Mr. Wirt. "Patrick spoke in this cause near an hour, and in a manner that surprised me. He showed himself well-informed upon a subject of which I did not think he had any knowledge."

"I have tried much," continues Mr. Wirt, "to procure a sketch of this celebrated speech. But those of Mr. Henry's hearers, who survive, seem to have been bereft of their senses. They can only tell you, in general, that they were taken captive, and were so delighted with their captivity, that they followed implicitly whithersoever he led them; that, at his bidding, their tears flowed from pity, and their cheeks flushed with indignation; that, when it was over, they felt as if they had just awaked from some ecstatic

dream, of which they were unable to recall or
connect the particulars. It was such a speech as
they believe had never before fallen from the lips
of man; and, to this day, the old people of that
county cannot conceive that a higher compliment
can be paid to a speaker, than to say of him, in
their own homely phrase, 'He is almost equal
to Patrick, when he plead against the parsons.'"

In this account of the character and effect of
Henry's argument, there is obviously a large
mixture of the poetical element, carried, in fact,
rather beyond the limits of good taste in the
forms of expression. The main facts are, however, of such a kind, that they cannot well have
been fabricated or misrepresented. The verdict
of the jury and the opinions of the court are
matters of record; the eager attention of the
audience during the argument, and the popular
triumph at the close, are quite in accordance with
the general character of the scene. The only
statement of fact that wears a rather doubtful
appearance is "the flight of the clergy in precipitation and terror from the bench." Whatever disgust or indignation may have been excited in their minds by the invectives of Henry,
there was no reason to apprehend any danger
to their personal safety.

The fact, probably, was that one or more,
possibly the whole body of the clergy, on

ascertaining the line of argument which he intended to pursue, retired from the bench, not in terror, but from unwillingness to listen to a furious attack on their own order. The irregularity of the proceeding does not seem to have been quite so great as Mr. Wirt represents it. He says, that the subject of the act of 1758, and the order of council respecting it, had been disposed of at the preceding term, and that, strictly speaking, neither Henry nor the jury had any thing to do with this part of the case; that the jury, in giving merely nominal damages, had lost sight, not only of the act of 1758, but of that of 1748, and of the admitted right of the plaintiff; and that the court, in overruling the motion for a new trial, showed that "they had lost the equipoise of their judgment." He can only account for such proceedings in part by the supposed laxity of the county court practice, and in part by the overwhelming effect of Henry's eloquence.

In reality, however, although the court had decided, at the preceding term, that the demurrer was good in law, it remained for the jury to settle, as a question of fact, the amount of damage actually suffered. Supposing the law to be with the clergy, substantial justice might still be on the other side; and in that case, the damage sustained by the clergy was of the kind described in the books as *damnum absque injuria* (damage without injury). In such a case, a verdict of nominal damages is obviously the proper one, the precise object of such a verdict being to recognize the existence of a legal right on one side, and an equitable one on the other; nor does it appear that the court had any sufficient motive for granting a new trial. The law question had been decided at the preceding term, agreeably to the views of the party making the motion, and, of course, did not require to be reconsidered. The verdict of the jury, whether right or wrong, was within the form of law, and was liable to no exception which would justify an application for a new trial.

The case, as I have remarked before, was a good deal stronger against the clergy than Mr. Wirt is inclined to represent it, and seems, on the whole, to have been disposed of, at every stage of the proceedings, in a manner very creditable to the firmness and independence of the parties to which it was successively submitted. The court, composed probably for the most part of planters, evinced a laudable disinterestedness in deciding the demurrer against themselves, and in favor of the clergy. The jury exhibited both intelligence and independence, in taking the course which enabled them to reconcile substantial justice with the form of law; and the court, in overruling the motion for a new trial, only carried into effect the common rules of proceeding.

It is highly probable, that the eloquence of Henry operated powerfully on the minds of the court and jury, as well as on those of the audience; but it is certain that its effect must have been greatly heightened by the strong sympathy, that prevailed throughout the community with the party which he supported, and the universal disposition of his hearers to receive with favor everything that he might say. Without intending any disparagement to his talents, we may perhaps conclude, with safety, that the strong excitement which existed in regard to the question at issue furnishes the true key to the more extravagant, and otherwise almost incredible, incidents that marked the proceedings in the trial of the Parsons' Cause. While it was in Henry a strong proof of real power, that, on appearing for the first time as an advocate, he was able to meet the exigencies of such a scene, it was also an instance of good fortune to have been called upon to make his *début* in a case in which he necessarily carried with him the full current of popular feeling, and thus to enter, under the most favorable auspices, upon his professional career. Without adverting to the extraordinary interest felt at the time in this case, it would be difficult to account for the fact, that, in the long course of his subsequent efforts in so many different fields, he never seems to have surpassed, if, indeed, he ever quite equalled, the impression, which he made upon this occasion, and that the argument in the Parsons' Cause is still cited as the *ne plus ultra* of his unrivalled eloquence.

Of the topics treated in this celebrated speech, the only one of which any account has been preserved, is that of the validity of the act of 1758, and of the proceedings respecting it by the king in council. Henry is represented by Mr. Wirt, on the authority, as I understand him, of oral tradition, as having maintained that government was in the nature of a compact between the king and the people; that the king, on failing to secure his subjects in Virginia against the results of a short crop of tobacco, had violated this compact, and thereby discharged the other party from the duty of executing it; and that the people had provided for their own safety by the act of 1758, the validity of which was in no way affected by the declaration of its nullity from the king in council. This is not, perhaps, the strongest form in which the argument on this topic could have been presented for the purpose which Henry had in view. It is not improbable that his reasoning may have been somewhat misrepresented in passing through the mouths of oral reporters. The object of Henry was to obtain a verdict of nominal damages, by showing that, wherever the legal right might be, substantial justice was on the side of the planters. In this purpose it was not necessary to argue, that the king was bound by the social compact to secure the Virginia planters against the results of a short crop of tobacco, which he could not well be expected to do, or that the order in council, annulling the act of 1758, had no legal validity. The natural course of the argument would be, that the clergy had no claim in justice to triple their salaries, at the expense of the planters, in consequence of an accidental rise in the value of a particular article; that, in founding such a claim upon a circumstance, which was in itself in the nature of a public calamity, the clergy acted inconsistently with their professional character; that the legislature, in securing the planters by law against such a pretension, proceeded in accordance with the dictates of natural justice; that, under the peculiar circumstances of the case, it was physically impossible to obtain the king's assent to the law, and that the legislature were consequently justified by necessity in proceeding without it; and that the subsequent declaration of the council, however it might affect the validity of the law, could not affect the equity of the case, nor consequently impair the right of the plaintiff to a verdict of merely nominal damages. This is the argument, which would naturally have been suggested by the aspect under which the case was presented. It is tenable in all its points, and only required to be stated with power and eloquence, in order to carry conviction to the mind of every hearer. The development of it would naturally include a course of severe animadversion on the conduct of the clergy, in seeking to fatten on the public distress; but it would not have been necessary to insist on any views of the law inconsistent with those, which had already been taken by the court. It may therefore be presumed, that it is the outline of the argument adopted by Henry.

Such is the history of the famous Parsons' Cause. The clergy took no steps for carrying the matter before a higher tribunal. Mr. Camm published another pamphlet, in which the *obscure advocate* of the planters, and the court in which the cause had been tried, were treated with great contempt. But the interest that had been for some time felt in this affair was immediately forgotten, under the stronger excitement produced by the opening scenes of the revolutionary contest, and left no results of consequence, excepting that of having brought before the public view, under the most favorable auspices, at this critical period, an individual better fitted, perhaps, by character and talents, than any other in the colony, to ride on the whirlwind and direct the storm.

Henry was at once retained for the planters in all the cases then in court, depending on the same principles with that of Mr. Maury; but they were all withdrawn by the clergy, and never came to trial. His business increased considerably, but was still for some time hardly adequate to his support; and, for the purpose of obtaining a wider field for his operations, he removed to the county of Louisa, where he resided at a place called the *Roundabout*. Here he resumed, in connection with his professional occupations, his favorite rural sports, and has been known to hunt the deer for several days together, carrying his provision with him, and at night encamping in the woods. After the hunt was over, he would go from the ground to the Louisa court-house in his hunting apparel, take up the first of his causes that happened to be called, and, if it afforded any scope for display, astonish the court and jury by the effusions of his natural eloquence. His power of enchaining the attention of his hearers is strikingly shown by a remark of Judge Lyons, the same person who had argued the Parsons' Cause against him, and who has been heard to say, that, while practising at the bar, he could always write a letter, or draft a legal paper, in court, with as much freedom of mind as in his own office, under all circumstances, excepting when *Patrick* rose to speak; but that, whenever this happened, however trifling might be the matter in question, he was obliged to throw aside his pen, and could not write a word until the speech was finished.

In the autumn of 1764, about a year after his argument in the Parsons' Cause, Henry was employed to appear before a committee of the House of Burgesses, in a case of a contested election, and acquitted himself with great distinction. But the moment had now arrived when he was himself to take his seat in the assembly, and for a time to govern its proceedings on the mighty questions in regard to which the colonies were at issue with the mother country.

CHAPTER III.

Elected a Member of the House of Burgesses. — Brings forward his celebrated Resolutions on the Stamp Act.

The year in which Patrick Henry argued the Parsons' Cause was distinguished by an event of high importance to the concerns of this continent, and ultimately, through them, of the whole Christian world. In that year were signed at Paris, by the representatives of the principal European powers, the definitive treaties which brought to a close the war of 1756, commonly called, in this country, the *Old French War*. By these treaties, France, then in the hands of the corrupt and imbecile administration, which governed in the name of Louis the Fifteenth, threw from her, as if in wantonness, the vast territory which she had previously possessed on this continent, and which, properly administered, might have secured to her the dominion of the whole. Canada was ceded to Great Britain. Louisiana, comprehending, as claimed by France, the entire valley of the Mississippi, from the mouth of that river to its sources, and from the Allegany to the Rocky Mountains, perhaps, on the whole, the richest and most favored region of equal extent on the face of the globe, was given away, as it seems, without any motive whatever, to Spain. By the same treaties, Florida was ceded by Spain to England.

It was doubtless supposed, at the time, that these arrangements had consolidated and established forever the dominion of Great Britain over the whole western continent. Occupying the coast from Davis's Straits to Cape Florida, relieved from the dangerous neighborhood of the French, who had hitherto in some degree kept them in check, and with nothing to oppose their farther progress but a torpid Spanish government at New Orleans, it was naturally supposed that the colonies would regularly and eagerly push forward their settlements into the interior, until they had driven the Spaniards from the continent; in short, that they would run, as British subjects, the same career, which they have, in fact, pursued as citizens of the United States.

This was the superficial aspect of the case; but a keener foresight into the future might, perhaps, even then have satisfied the observer that the result of these arrangements would be of a directly opposite character, and would tend to weaken and dismember, rather than consolidate and strengthen, the British power. The neighborhood of the French was the principal circumstance that counteracted this tendency to independence, which naturally grew out of the remote situation of the British colonies, and their peculiar habits of thought and feeling. At the occurrence of every new war in Europe, the British settlements in America were exposed to new inroads from the interior, aggravated in their effects by all the horrors of savage warfare. The necessity of obtaining the aid of the mother country in repelling these attacks, and the sympathy generated by the concert of action thus produced, created, for the time, a community of feeling, which could never have been produced in any other way. The acquisition of Canada removed this check to the spirit of independence; and it might, perhaps, have been anticipated that this spirit would now develop itself with greater assurance and freedom than before. But even in this view of the subject, no contemporary observer would ever have predicted the rapidity, with which the new combination of circumstances produced its effects. At no period in the history of the colonies had the feeling on their part towards the mother country been so cordial, as it was at the conclusion of the peace of 1763. Twelve years afterwards, the mother country and the colonies were at open war; in thirteen, the colonies had declared independence; and in twenty, the representatives of the same powers, that made the arrangements of 1763, signed, at Paris, another set of treaties, the principal result of which was to recognize the national existence of the United States. So rapid, in some cases at least, is the progress of the revolutions which determine the fortunes of nations, and change the face of the world.

The event, which immediately brought on this new and wholly unexpected series of occurrences, took place in England in the year following the peace, and was one of its results. Desiring to make the reductions in the taxes, that are usual after the close of a long war, and finding it necessary at the same time to provide for the interest of a large war debt, the British ministry, in order to combine the two objects as far as possible, began to look about for new sources of revenue, and conceived the idea of raising funds by taxing the colonies. In pursuance of this project, on the 10th of March, 1764, a declaratory resolution was adopted in Parliament, to the effect, that it "would be proper to impose certain stamp duties on the colonies and plantations, for the purpose of raising an American revenue, payable into the British exchequer." At the next session of Parliament, in the year 1765, a law was passed, in conformity with this resolution, commonly called the Stamp Act.

The resolution and the act, though adopted by large majorities, were opposed in Parliament by a respectable minority, chiefly on the ground of constitutional law. The right of the government to raise money from the people by taxation was declared to be coëxtensive with, and incidental to, the right of the people to be represented in Parliament. As the colonies were not represented in Parliament, they could not rightfully be taxed. The correctness of this principle, even in its application to the mother country, may, perhaps, be regarded as somewhat questionable. With the inhabitants of the British islands, the right of being directly represented in Parliament is far from being, or having been at any time, coëxtensive with the duty of paying taxes; and the idea of virtual representation, it was supposed, might as well be applied to the population of the colonies, as to the unrepresented part of that of the mother country.

It may be urged, indeed, with some degree of plausibility, that, where the legislator is himself subject to his own laws, there is less danger of oppression than where they are made applicable only to a distant country. But this is a consideration of equity and expediency, rather than of strict right. In reality, the constitutional rights of British subjects, which at home depended on usage rather than strict definition, became, in the anomalous circumstances under which the colonies were settled, so entirely matters of inference and construction, that they must necessarily have been interpreted differently, and with almost equal degrees of plausibility, by the colonies and the government. It was the true policy of the government to avoid every thing that would provoke discussion on the subject, since, whatever the merits of the case might be, any agitation of the question would necessarily stimulate the existing tendency to independence.

The error of the British ministry lay in assuming a principle, which, whether in itself true or false, could not fail, at all events, to provoke a controversy, and in not retracing their steps with sufficient firmness, when they saw how the act was received in America.

Starting from the period of the peace of 1763, when the feeling of cordiality toward the mother country was strong and universal, had the British ministry pursued uniformly a conciliatory course, never advancing any pretension which was fitted to alarm the jealousy of the colonies, encouraging, instead of crushing, their home industry, governing them, in short, not with a view to the separate aggrandizement of Great Britain, but to the interest of the colonies themselves, and that of the mother country only as therein involved and implied; had the ministry taken such a course, the union with Great Britain might have lasted for an indefinite period, perhaps for centuries, and until the superior population and revenues of the colonies should have transferred the seat of the common government, by a natural process, to this side of the Atlantic. But such results would have been hardly consistent with the ordinary course of events. With the feelings on both sides that naturally grew out of their respective positions, it was much more natural that the British government should adopt some such measure as the stamp act, and that its adoption should be followed by resistance from the colonies.

But although opposition, more or less energetic, was naturally to be expected, and was doubtless calculated on by the ministers, it is hardly probable that they anticipated the storm of resistance which burst upon them at once from all quarters of the continent. The declaratory resolution was met by remonstrances and protests from the colonial legislatures, transmitted through their agents at London, in which they denied entirely the right of the government to raise a revenue from the colonies. Shaken in some degree by their proceedings, the ministry intimated to the agents that they had no particular predilection for the proposed method of raising the money wanted, and that they would abandon the idea of laying stamp duties if the agents would suggest any other mode of obtaining the amount which these duties were expected to yield, and which was only a hundred thousand pounds. So trifling was the pecuniary interest actually at stake in the quarrel, which was destined to dismember the British empire. The agents rejected these overtures, and insisted firmly on the constitutional right of British subjects not to be taxed excepting with their own consent through their representatives.

Failing in these attempts at conciliation, the ministry adhered to their original plan. Soon after the opening of Parliament, in January, 1765, they carried through the two Houses, by unanimous consent, a resolution not to receive any memorials which denied the right of the government to tax the colonies; and soon after proposed, and carried by large majorities, the famous stamp act. On the actual passage of this obnoxious law, the feeling of discontent which had been kept in some degree within bounds, by the hope that Parliament would refrain from following out the course indicated by the resolution of the preceding session, now burst forth with uncontrollable fury. On the arrival of the intelligence of the passage of the law at Boston, the ships in port displayed their flags at half mast as signals of distress; the bells were muffled and tolled as at a funeral. The act was publicly burned. The ship-masters who had brought out the stamps were compelled to give them up, and they were immediately destroyed, so that, on the 1st of November, when the act went into operation, there was not one to be found in the colonies.

The merchants entered into mutual compacts not to import any goods from Great Britain while the law remained in force. As the use of stamped paper was rendered necessary by the act in almost all matters of business, public or private, the destruction of the supply, which had been transmitted, interrupted the progress of all current affairs. The courts of justice were closed, and the people were left at full leisure to devote their whole time and attention to the all-absorbing subject. The rapidity with which the feeling that prevailed through the colonies changed, in a single year, from unprecedented cordiality to unmitigated abhorrence, is almost miraculous. It evinces a keen sensibility to any interference with their real or supposed political rights, and a resolute determination to maintain them, singularly characteristic of the race from which they sprang, but which had never, perhaps, been displayed with greater energy at the most trying periods in the history of the mother country.

The legislature of Virginia, immediately after receiving intelligence of the adoption of the declaratory resolution by Parliament, prepared addresses, directed severally to the King, the House of Lords, and the House of Commons, in which they remonstrated with spirit and decision, but still in a tone of moderation, against any actual legislation on this basis. These addresses corresponded in character with the feeling which prevailed in the colonies at the time of their adoption, and which was still friendly and loyal

towards the mother country, although in some
degree altered by the prospect of the measures
that were threatened. The actual passage of the
stamp act seems to have obliterated entirely the
remains of the previously existing sentiment, and
to have substituted in its place the most intense
excitement, and a resolute determination to resist
to the utmost, and at all hazards, the ministerial
pretensions. The boldest and most energetic
patriots were naturally called into action by the
nature of the crisis.

In Virginia, the friends of liberty fixed their
eyes immediately upon the young advocate, who
had recently acquired so much reputation by his
brilliant eloquence and undaunted defence of
colonial rights against the encroachments of the
crown, at the regular election of members of the
House of Burgesses for the year 1765. Henry
does not seem to have been thought of as a
candidate; but, after the adoption of the stamp
act was known, Mr. William Johnson, the
member elect for the county of Louisa, accepted
the place of coroner in order to create a vacancy.
A writ was issued on the 1st of May for a new
election, and before the 20th it appears that
Henry had taken his seat in the Assembly, which
was in session at the time, as on that day he
was added to the committee for courts of justice.
On making his appearance in the Assembly, he

exhibited the same plain and rather uncouth exterior which had previously distinguished him. It now formed a rather striking contrast with the stately deportment and finished elegance of manner, which characterized the leading members of the landed aristocracy of Virginia.

It was probably not anticipated by the friends of Henry, that he would lead the proceedings of the Assembly on the stamp act. Richard Henry Lee, Pendleton, Wythe, Bland, and others, who afterwards took an active and prominent part in the contest with the mother country, were members of this body, and, from their superiority in years and authority, if not in talent and eloquence, to Henry, were naturally expected to assume the responsibility of pointing out the course to be pursued. Henry, as a young and powerful advocate, was calculated on to sustain and recommend to the people the measures proposed by the leaders. These very natural expectations were, as we shall presently see, entirely disappointed.

The first affair in which Henry took a part was far from exhibiting any very strong tendency in him to follow the lead of the landed aristocracy. Although it had no immediate connection with the exciting political topics of the day, it was in itself of an interesting character, and, in more quiet times, would have probably absorbed for some years the attention of the colony. It was a proposal made in the Assembly to convert the state treasury into a sort of land bank, by authorizing the treasurer to lend the public money to individuals on good landed security. Whether these loans were to be made in a paper money, resting on the public faith, to be created for the purpose, or in the usual currency of the colony, is not stated in the accounts that have come down to us of this transaction.

The treasurer of the colony at this period was John Robinson, who was also at the same time, and had been for five and twenty years preceding, the speaker of the Assembly. He was a person of large property and excellent character, by general acknowledgment the leader of the landed interest. Profuse in his expenditures, and liberal in his disposition, he had been in the habit of lending money very freely to such persons as wished to borrow, employing indiscriminately, for this purpose, his own funds and those of the state. By a long perseverance in this system his affairs had become confused, and he began to apprehend that he should find himself unable to meet his payments on public account. The real object of the proposed measure was to enable him to settle his affairs, by transferring the loans which he had made on his own responsibility, though with the public money, to the credit of the state. As the irregularity of the manner in which Robinson had managed the affairs of the treasury was not known until after his death, which took place a year later, the real object of the proposed measure was not at the time suspected by the public. The plan seems to have been favored by the leading members of the Assembly, who naturally anticipated that the loans to be made would fall, in part at least, into their hands.

It was in opposition to this plan that Henry made his first speech in the House of Burgesses. The ultimate object not being known, he could, of course, attack it only on the general ground of objections, which are sufficiently obvious; such as the danger, inconvenience, and radical impropriety, of employing the public money in private banking operations, and the abuses to which such a system would necessarily lead. No report is extant of this speech. Mr. Jefferson, who heard the debate, speaks of it as an effort of great ability, and quotes a single remark, which made at the time a very strong impression on himself and the House. It had been urged by the friends of the measure, that certain persons of substantial property had been led by circumstances to contract debts, which, if exacted immediately, would bring ruin upon them and their families, but that, with a little indulgence in point of time, these debts might be paid with ease, and that this project would furnish the persons so situated with the accommodation which they wanted. "What, Sir," said Henry, in commenting upon this remark, which seems to have been a covert allusion to the case of Robinson himself; "What, Sir, is it proposed, then, to reclaim the spendthrift from his dissipation and extravagance by filling his pockets with money?" "These expressions," says Jefferson, in his letter to Wirt, "are indelibly impressed upon my memory." As the remark here quoted, though just and pointed, has nothing particularly striking or brilliant about it, it is easy to judge how much the effect of Henry's speeches, as is the case, indeed, with those of every celebrated orator, must have depended on the manner in which they were delivered. The opposition of Henry to the projected plan was successful. He carried with him all the members of the upper country, who constituted a considerable majority over the aristocracy of the lower country.

The next year Robinson died, and the disclosure of the deficit in his accounts with the state, which exhibited the true character of this proposal, fully justifies the opposition of Henry, and reflected honor on his foresight and sagacity. He assumed at this time the position, which he continued to hold through his whole career, of a popular tribune, who made it his business to attempt to secure the rights of the mass of the community against invasion by the wealthy and powerful. This might not have been, in ordinary times, a course very well fitted to secure to him the highest emoluments and advantages held out by his profession, as it naturally rendered him obnoxious to the landed proprietors, who owned most of the property, and disposed of all the patronage of the crown in the colony. But, under the peculiar circumstances of the crisis, it proved perhaps more favorable to his influence than any other that he could have adopted. The progress of events very soon transferred the patronage of the colony from the hands of the aristocracy to those of the popular leaders, and compelled the former not merely not to oppose Henry, but to march, though not with a very good will, under his banner. This result was seen in the proceedings of the Assembly at this session upon the stamp act.

The leading men appear to have made up their minds, that it was unnecessary to add anything, at this session, to the addresses which had been adopted at the preceding one, and, up to the third day before the session was to terminate, had shown no intention to propose any new measure. It was at this period that Henry introduced his celebrated resolutions. At some subsequent time, he made, himself, a statement in writing of the circumstances under which they were offered. The document is the more curious, as it is the only source from which our knowledge of one of the resolutions is derived. After the decease of Henry, a parcel was found among his papers, with this superscription; "Enclosed are the resolutions of the Virginia Assembly, in 1765, concerning the stamp act. Let my executors open this paper." The parcel contained a copy of the resolutions, with some remarks written upon the back of it, the whole in Henry's hand-writing. The resolutions are as follows;

"Resolved, That the first adventurers and settlers of this his Majesty's colony and dominion brought with them, and transmitted to their posterity, and all others, his Majesty's subjects, since inhabiting in this his Majesty's said colony, all the privileges, franchises, and immunities, that have at any time been held, enjoyed, and possessed, by the people of Great Britain.

"Resolved, That, by two royal charters, granted by King James the First, the colonists aforesaid are declared entitled to all the privileges, liberties, and immunities of denizens and natural-born subjects, to all intents and purposes, as if they had been abiding and born within the realm of England.

"Resolved, That the taxation of the people

by themselves, or by persons chosen by themselves to represent them, who can only know what taxes the people are able to bear, and the easiest mode of raising them, and are equally affected by such taxes themselves, is the distinguishing characteristic of British freedom, and without which the ancient constitution cannot subsist.

"Resolved, That his Majesty's liege people of this most ancient colony have uninterruptedly enjoyed the right of being thus governed by their own Assembly, in the article of their taxes and internal police; and that the same hath never been forfeited, or any other way given up, but hath been constantly recognized by the king and people of Great Britain.

" Resolved, therefore, That the General Assembly of this colony have the sole right and power to lay taxes and impositions upon the inhabitants of this colony; and that every attempt to vest such power in any person or persons whatsoever, other than the General Assembly aforesaid, has a manifest tendency to destroy British, as well as American, freedom."

The endorsement, also in Henry's hand-writing, on the paper containing these resolutions, is as follows;

"The within resolutions passed the House of Burgesses in May, 1765. They formed the first opposition to the stamp act, and the scheme of taxing America by the British Parliament. All the colonies, either through fear or want of opportunity to form an opposition, or from influences of some kind or other, had remained silent. I had been, for the first time, elected a burgess a few days before; was young, inexperienced, unacquainted with the forms of the House, and the members that composed it. Finding the men of weight averse to opposition, and the commencement of the tax at hand, and that no person was likely to step forth, I determined to venture; and, alone, unadvised, on a blank leaf of an old law book, wrote the within. Upon offering them to the House, violent debates ensued. Many threats were uttered, and much abuse cast on me by the party for submission. After a long and warm contest, the resolutions passed by a very small majority, perhaps of one or two only. The alarm spread throughout America with astonishing quickness, and the ministerial party were overwhelmed. The great point of resistance to British taxation was universally established in the colonies. This brought on the war, which finally separated the two countries, and gave independence to ours. Whether this will prove a blessing or a curse, will depend upon the use our people make of the blessings which a gracious God hath bestowed upon us.

If they are wise, they will be great and happy. If they are of a contrary character, they will be miserable. Righteousness alone can exalt them as a nation.

"Reader! whoever thou art, remember this; and, in thy sphere, practise virtue thyself, and encourage it in others. P. HENRY."

Such is the account, given by Henry himself, of the passage of these resolutions. It is known, also, from himself, through the channel of his brother-in-law, Judge Winston, that, before they were offered, they were shown to two persons only, John Fleming and George Johnston, members respectively for the counties of Cumberland and Fairfax, by the latter of whom they were seconded. They were opposed, with great earnestness by the prominent members, who generally led the proceedings, and, on most occasions, as a matter of course, commanded a majority. The reader will naturally desire to see the account of the proceedings, as given in the graphic and spirited language of Jefferson, who was present at the debate.

"Mr. Henry moved, and Mr. Johnston seconded, these resolutions, successively. They were opposed by Messrs. Randolph, Bland, Pendleton, Wythe, and all the old members, whose influence in the House had till then been unbroken. They did it, not from any question of our rights, but on the ground that the same sentiments had been, at the preceding session, expressed in a more conciliatory form, to which the answers were not yet received. But torrents of sublime eloquence from Henry, backed by the solid reasoning of Johnston, prevailed. The last, however, and strongest resolution, was carried but by a single vote. The debate on it was most bloody. I was then but a student, and stood at the door of communication between the house and the lobby, (for as yet there was no gallery,) during the whole debate and vote; and I well remember, that, after the numbers on the division were told and declared from the chair, Peyton Randolph, the attorney-general, came out at the door where I was standing, and said, as he entered the lobby, 'I would have given five hundred guineas for a single vote;' for one vote would have divided the house, and Robinson was in the chair, who, he knew, would have negatived the resolution.

"Mr. Henry left town that evening; and the next morning, before the meeting of the House, Colonel Peter Randolph, then of the council, came to the hall of burgesses, and sat at the clerk's table till the house bell rang, thumbing over the volumes of journals, to find a precedent for expunging a vote of the House, which, he said, had taken place while he was a member or clerk of the House, I do not recollect which. I stood by him, at the end of the table, a considerable part of the time, looking on as he turned the leaves; but I do not recollect whether he found the erasure. In the mean time, some of the timid members, who had voted for the strongest resolution, had become alarmed; and, as soon as the House met, a motion was made and carried to expunge it from the journals. There being, at that day, but one printer, and he entirely under control of the governor, I do not know that this resolution ever appeared in print. I write this from memory; but the impression made on me, at the time, was such as to fix the facts indelibly in my mind. I suppose the original journal was among those destroyed by the British, or its obliterated face might be appealed to. And here I will state, that Burk's statement of Mr. Henry's consenting to withdraw two resolutions, by way of compromise with his opponents, is entirely erroneous."

Mr. Jefferson's suggestion, that the manuscript journal was probably destroyed by the British during the war, has been ascertained to be erroneous, as the book disappeared very soon after the close of the session of 1765. There are various errors, besides the one mentioned by Mr. Jefferson, in the account of Burk, and some in that of Marshall, in the first volume of the Life of Washington. Fortunately, the original note of Henry, and the account of Jefferson, enable us to form a perfectly correct, as well as singularly clear and distinct, notion of this thrilling scene. Jefferson standing as a listener at the door of the House of Burgesses, and imbibing, from the "torrents of Henry's sublime eloquence," the patriotic inspiration, which was destined, only ten years afterwards, to glow in his own draft of the Declaration of Independence, would furnish a noble subject for the historical painter, and one which would open plainly to the eye some of the powerful, but then hidden, springs of the coming revolution.

Of the speech or speeches made by Henry in this debate, there is no satisfactory record. Burk, in his History, gives what purports to be his speech; but it is the mere outline of an argument, resting, probably, on recollection, with the exception of a single passage at the close, the correctness of which is well authenticated, and which contributed greatly, at the time, by giving effect and poignancy to the whole speech, to produce the desired result. According to this outline, Henry considered the pretence of the ministry to raise a revenue in this country as conflicting with the colonial charters, with the rights of the people as British subjects, and with their natural rights as men. At the close, he dwelt upon the danger to which the king himself would be exposed, in pursuing his present course. "Cæsar," said he, "had his Brutus, Charles the First his Cromwell, and George the Third —" At this moment, the orator paused, as if in doubt how to finish the sentence. The natural termination seemed, of course, to be, that George the Third would come, like them, to a violent end; and the members opposed to Henry immediately raised a loud cry of "Treason, treason," in all parts of the house. Henry, in no way disconcerted, but appearing, on the contrary, to gather new power from the excitement of the scene, assumed a more erect position, and, fastening his eagle eye upon the speaker, the same John Robinson, whose corrupt plans he had so signally baffled a few days before, added, in the most appropriate emphasis, as the closing words of the phrase, "may profit by their example." He then paused again, for some seconds, and finally subjoined, as a sort of commentary on the outcry that had just occurred, "If this be treason, make the most of it."

Such was the first appearance of Henry as an orator on purely political topics; and it is a rather singular circumstance, that, in this department, as in that of legal practice, no subsequent effort seems to have surpassed, or even quite equalled, in immediate effect, the first. His speech in the Continental Congress, soon after its organization, called forth the strongest admiration; many of his speeches in the Virginia Convention, on the federal constitution, were received with unbounded enthusiasm, and produced very extraordinary results. His argument in the British Debt case, which occupied three days, is analyzed at great length by Mr. Wirt, and dwelt upon as a sort of masterpiece. But, even at the present time, a Virginian, who is requested to mention the leading titles of Henry's glory, appeals, without hesitation, to the speeches on the Stamp Act and the Parsons' Cause. The peculiar circumstances attending each of these cases may have contributed something to give them their comparative importance; but, independently of any other cause, there is a certain freshness in the first efforts of a powerful mind, which gives them an advantage over those of later years, that, on careful analysis, may appear, as works of science and art, fully equal, if not superior.

It is remarked by Lord Byron, in one of his private memoranda or letters, that he awoke one morning and found himself famous. Henry had taken his seat in the Assembly, notwithstanding the eclat of the Parsons' Cause, a still comparatively obscure country attorney, at best a rising lawyer of great promise. He returned to his home, three or four weeks after, by universal acknowledgment, the first statesman and orator in Virginia.

CHAPTER IV.

Repeal of the Stamp Act. — Henry elected to the Continental Congress. — Speech in the Virginia Convention.

The unfortunate measure, which had produced such a ferment throughout the colonies, and which exercised so important an influence on their relations with the mother country, was destined itself to be of short duration. Within a year after the passage of the stamp act, a change took place in the administration of the British government. The Grenville cabinet, in which the tory influence predominated, was compelled to retire; and a new one was formed, on whig principles, under the direction of the Marquis of Rockingham. It was on this occasion that Burke, who had previously been private secretary to the marquis, took his seat in Parliament. It may be proper to remark, that, although the Grenville administration was ostensibly responsible for the passage of the stamp act, Mr. Grenville himself is said to have been individually averse to it, and to have proposed it very unwillingly, in compliance with the positive command of the king, who was the real author of the measure. However this may be, the new ministry, who, as members of Parliament, had opposed the adoption of this policy, very naturally evinced a disposition to recede from it. The speech from the throne, at the opening of the session, breathed a conciliatory spirit in regard to America; and, in the debate upon it in the House of Commons, Mr. Pitt attacked the policy of the late administration with great power. A bill was introduced, soon after, for the repeal of the stamp act, which, though strongly opposed, passed the two Houses by large majorities, and became a law. At the same time, another law was passed, declaratory of the right of Parliament to bind the colonies in all cases whatsoever.

This prompt and apparently good-humored retreat from the course, which had been so injudiciously entered upon, gave entire satisfaction throughout the colonies, and restored for a moment the cordial feeling towards the mother country, that prevailed at the close of the war. Public rejoicings, including expressions of the warmest gratitude to the friends of the colonies, at home and abroad, took place in all quarters. The Virginia Assembly voted an address of thanks to the King and Parliament, in which they renewed all their former professions of attachment and loyalty. They also resolved to erect a statue of the King, and an obelisk in honor of the British statesmen who had supported the cause of America. A bill was introduced for this purpose; but, in consequence of the less favorable aspect which the affair shortly after assumed in England, it was never acted on.

Had the British government, at this period, persevered, with consistency and good faith, in the policy which apparently dictated the repeal of the stamp act, there can be no doubt, that the good feeling produced by that repeal would have been maintained, and would have prevailed for a long time in the relations between the two parties. But this was not the case; and the course actually pursued was one which it would be as difficult to reconcile with any consistent scheme of administration, as with a prudent regard to the rights and feelings of the colonies.

Occasional concessions gave an appearance of weakness and indecision to the action of the ministry, while the extreme severity displayed on other occasions irritated the minds of the

Americans almost to frenzy. Not content with annexing to the repeal of the stamp act a declaratory law, which was fitted of itself to give an ungracious aspect to the whole proceeding, the ministry seem to have taken particular pains to disavow any intention for which the colonies could properly be grateful, and publicly treated with contempt the demonstrations of satisfaction which had, in fact, been shown in America. Townshend, the new chancellor of the exchequer, remarked, in a speech made the following year, in the debate on the supplies, "that he had voted for the repeal of the stamp act, not because it was not a good act, but because there appeared to be a propriety in repealing it. He added, that he repeated the sentiment in order that the galleries might hear him; and that, after this, he did not expect to have his statue erected in America." In accordance with these views, the plan of raising a revenue in the colonies was immediately revived. A law was passed, the same year, imposing new duties upon various articles, when imported into the colonies, and particularly *tea*; and, in order to show the settled determination of the ministry to persist, at all hazards, in their pretensions, additional troops were sent to America, and quartered in the principal northern cities.

This headstrong spirit in the cabinet could

not well produce any other results than such as those which followed, and which are familiarly known as a part of the general history of the country. Virginia, though prominent in resistance to the stamp act, seems to have been treated with less severity than some of the other colonies. This is attributed, by Mr. Wirt, to the personal character of the Virginian governors, Fauquier and Botetourt, who are represented as having endeavored to maintain, as far as possible, a good understanding between the parties; while it seems to have been the object of the Bernards and Hutchinsons, of the eastern states, to envenom existing animosities, and push them as rapidly as possible to extremities. The greater consideration, which was extended by the mother country to the colony of Virginia, tended probably to diminish a little, on her side, the activity of opposition.

On the repeal of the stamp act, the Assembly, as remarked above, adopted resolutions of a highly loyal character; and it does not appear that any new proceedings took place in reference to the relations with the mother country until the session of 1768-9. On the last day of that session, a series of resolutions was adopted, asserting in emphatic terms the right of the colony to be exempt from all taxes excepting such as might be imposed by her own legislature, and remonstrating vigorously against the recent acts of the British government. The result of this measure was an immediate dissolution of the House of Assembly by the governor. The members were all reëlected, and returned with augmented ardor to the post of duty. The next step, in the course of resistance to the arbitrary pretensions of the ministry, was the adoption by the Assembly of a series of resolutions, moved by Dabney Carr, and providing for the appointment of a committee of the legislature to correspond with the legislatures of the other colonies. The measure was moved in committee of the whole on the 12th of March, 1773, and was the first movement made in any part of the country towards a concert of action between the colonies.

Henry had constantly been a member of the House from the time of his first election, and took, no doubt, an active part on both these occasions, although no particular account has been preserved of his course in regard to the resolutions of 1768–9. He supported those of Mr. Carr in a powerful speech, and was appointed a member of the Committee of Correspondence. He seems, at this time, to have become somewhat more studious, in regard to the decorum of his external appearance, than he had formerly been; and is described by one who was present at the debate on Carr's resolutions as wearing a peach-blossom-colored coat, and dark wig, terminating in a bag, according to the fashion of that day. He was now in full practice at the bar, and was particularly conspicuous in the defence of criminal cases, where he shone without a rival. In civil actions, involving the technical book learning of the profession, he was still unable to cope on equal terms with the leading barristers, and only recovered his advantage, and displayed his full strength, when the question was of such a nature that he was at liberty to appeal to the great principles of natural justice.

But events of high importance were now succeeding each other with a rapidity, which left to those who took an active part in political affairs but little leisure for professional pursuits or private business of any description. The attempt to enforce the new duty on tea was met by the destruction of the first cargo that arrived at Boston, while yet on board the ship in which it came. In retribution for this act of summary justice, the British government withdrew from that town its privileges as a port of entry, by the law commonly called the Boston Port Bill. The situation of Boston under this infliction called forth public expressions of the warmest sympathy from various quarters. The Virginia legislature was in session at the time when intelligence of the enactment of the Boston Port Bill reached this country. The bill was to take effect on the first of June, 1774. The Assembly immediately passed an order setting apart that day to be observed as a season of public fasting, humiliation, and prayer. In consequence of this order, Governor Dunmore on the following day dissolved the House. The members forthwith repaired to the Raleigh tavern, and, after deliberating on the course which it was proper to pursue under existing circumstances, unanimously adopted an Association, which contained a proposal for the meeting of a General Congress.

In pursuance of these proceedings, delegates were elected shortly after by the several counties, to meet, on the 1st of August following, for the purpose of considering further of the state of public affairs, and particularly of appointing deputies to the General Congress. The delegates accordingly assembled at Williamsburg, at the appointed time, and proceeded to transact the business committed to them. They adopted resolutions, in which they pledge themselves to make common cause with Boston at all hazards, and to suspend all commercial intercourse with Great Britain, until the existing difficulties should be adjusted. As deputies to the General Congress they designated Peyton Randolph, Richard

Henry Lee, George Washington, Patrick Henry, Richard Bland, Benjamin Harrison, and Edmund Pendleton. The president of the Convention, Peyton Randolph, was authorized to call another meeting, if occasion should require.

Notwithstanding the lengths to which the controversy with the mother country had now proceeded, and the bitterness of feeling which had been generated by it, the idea of complete independence was still admitted with reluctance by the greater part of even the more active patriots, and had not become familiar to the people at large. A few persons only, of deeper thought and a keener foresight into future events than the rest, already perceived that this result was inevitable. Patrick Henry was one of the number, and Mr. Wirt has recorded a very interesting conversation that occurred about this time, in which Henry developed his views, with his characteristic boldness, and with almost prophetic sagacity; the substance of which is here related.

The conversation was held at the house of Colonel Samuel Overton, who, in the presence of several other gentlemen, inquired of Henry whether he supposed that Great Britain would drive her colonies to extremities; and, if so, what would be the issue of the war. "Sir," said Henry in reply, after looking round the company to see that none but confidential persons were present, "she will drive us to extremities; no accommodation will take place; hostilities will soon commence, and a desperate and bloody contest it will be." "Do you think," continued Overton, "that, destitute as we are of arms, ammunition, ships of war, and money to procure them, we can possibly make any effectual resistance to the forces which Great Britain will send against us?" "To be candid with you," replied Henry, "I doubt whether we should be able to cope single-handed with so formidable an adversary; but," continued he, rising from his seat, with great vivacity, "do you suppose that France, Spain, and Holland, the natural enemies of Great Britain, will look on quietly and see us crushed? Will Louis the Sixteenth be asleep at such a crisis? No, Sir! When he shall be satisfied, by the vigor of our resistance, and by our *declaration of independence*, that we are in earnest, he will furnish us with supplies, send us fleets and armies to fight our battles for us, and make a treaty, offensive and defensive, with us against our unnatural mother. Spain and Holland will join the alliance; our independence will be established, and we shall take our place among the nations of the earth."

On the 5th of September, 1774, the deputies to the General Congress met at Carpenter's Hall, in Philadelphia. Peyton Randolph was chosen president. After the formal organization had been completed, the proceedings were opened by a speech from Henry, which was followed by another from Richard Henry Lee. No report of these speeches has been preserved, but they are represented by Mr. Wirt, on the authority of those who heard them, as having been in the highest degree powerful and impressive. Committees were shortly after appointed to prepare a petition to the king, an address to the people of England, and another to the inhabitants of British America. In consequence of their general reputation, as well as of the splendid display of eloquence which they had already made, Henry and Lee were intrusted respectively with the duty of preparing the first and second of these documents. It appeared, however, in the sequel, that the capacity of these gentlemen for literary composition and regular argument was not upon a level with their gift in speech. The drafts which they reported gave, in both cases, so little satisfaction, that they were recommitted, and others substituted for them, the petition to the king having been drafted by Mr. Jay, and the address to the people of England by Mr. Dickinson.

Judge Chase, of Maryland, who was a member of this Congress, on hearing the first speeches of

Henry and Lee, walked across the floor to the seat of his colleague, and said to him, in an under tone, "We may as well go home; we are not able to legislate with these men." After their talent for transacting the public affairs had been tested, the judge was heard to remark, "I find, after all, they are but men, and, in mere matters of business, but very common men."

No account has been preserved of any further proceedings of Henry in this Congress, which closed its sittings in October. On his return home, Henry was, of course, surrounded by his neighbors, who were eager to learn the particulars of the debates, and inquired, among other things, whom he thought the greatest man in Congress. "If you speak of eloquence," replied Henry, "Mr. Rutledge, of South Carolina, is by far the greatest orator; but if you speak of solid information and sound judgment, Colonel Washington is unquestionably the greatest man on that floor." Washington, though still comparatively young, had already developed, in a protracted career of service, his eminent capacity for military affairs, and the practical despatch of business; he had been for many years a member of the Assembly, and had exhibited, under all circumstances, and on various trying occasions, the moral elevation of character, which was the great secret of his subsequent influence and success.

On the 20th of March, 1775, the Virginia Convention, which had met the preceding year at Williamsburg, came together, for the second time, at Richmond. Henry was a member of this body. It has already been remarked, that the public opinion and feeling throughout the colonies were not yet prepared for a declaration of independence. This was evinced, so far as Virginia was concerned, by the terms of the instructions given by the Williamsburg Convention to their deputies in Congress, which, in connection with a vigorous and plain-spoken statement of grievances, breathe a spirit of loyalty to the king and attachment to the mother country.

A similar tone marked the proceedings of the Congress itself; and, when the Williamsburg Convention met for the second time, the prevailing sentiment among the members was apparently pacific and conciliatory. The two first days were employed in passing resolves of a merely formal and complimentary character in honor of the deputies to Congress, and of the legislature of Jamaica, which had presented a petition to the king in favor of the claims of the colonies. These proceedings appeared to Henry altogether too tame for the exigencies of the crisis. He had made up his mind that the time for conciliation was over, and that the controversy had reached the point, where there was no other issue but an appeal to actual force. Preparation for the military defence of the colony was, of course, in this view, the only appropriate measure, and Henry conceived that the activity of the Convention ought to take this direction. He accordingly moved the following resolutions;

"Resolved, That a well-regulated militia, composed of gentlemen and yeomen, is the natural strength and only security of a free government; that such a militia in this colony would for ever render it unnecessary for the mother country to keep among us, for the purpose of our defence, any standing army of mercenary soldiers, always subversive of the quiet and dangerous to the liberties of the people, and would obviate the pretext of taxing us for their support.

"That the establishment of such a militia is at this time peculiarly necessary, by the state of our laws, for the protection and defence of the country, some of which are already expired, and others will shortly be so; and that the known remissness of government, in calling us together in a legislative capacity, renders it too insecure, in this time of danger and distress, to rely that opportunity will be given of renewing them in General Assembly, or making any provision to secure our inestimable rights and liberties from those further violations with which they are threatened.

"Resolved, therefore, That this colony be immediately put into a state of defence, and that a committee be raised to prepare a plan for imbodying, arming, and disciplining such a number of men as may be sufficient for that purpose."

On this occasion, as in the debate on the Stamp Act, the views of Henry were not only far in advance of the general sentiment of the country, but went beyond those of the most active patriots in the Convention. Bland, Harrison, and Pendleton, who had been members of Congress, with Robert C. Nicholas, one of the ablest and most respected citizens, resisted with all their might the passage of these resolutions. They urged, in opposition to them, with great eloquence, the more conciliatory temper that had lately been professed by the king and his ministers, the utter hopelessness of a contest with Great Britain, the intimate and endearing character of the ties that had hitherto connected the colonies with the mother country, and the advantages of various kinds which had accrued to both the parties from the connection.

It is apparent, from the arguments which they employed, that these eminent statesmen and patriots still clung with confidence to the hope of preserving the union. Henry replied to their arguments, and sustained his resolutions in a speech which is given by Mr. Wirt in a report furnished by Judge Tucker, who heard it delivered. This is one of the most powerful specimens, that have come down to us, of Henry's eloquence. It is inserted here from the report of Judge Tucker, with the substitution of the first for the third person.

"No man can think more highly than I do of the patriotism, as well as abilities, of the very worthy gentlemen who have just addressed the House. But different men often see the same subject in different lights; and, therefore, I hope it will not be thought disrespectful to those gentlemen, if, entertaining, as I do, opinions of a character very opposite to theirs, I shall speak forth my sentiments freely, and without reserve. This is no time for ceremony. The question before the House is one of awful moment to the country. For my own part, I consider it as nothing less than a question of freedom or slavery. And in proportion to the magnitude of the subject ought to be the freedom of the debate. It is only in this way that we can hope to arrive at truth, and fulfil the great responsibility which we hold to God and our country. Should I keep back my opinions at such a time, through fear of giving offence, I should consider myself as guilty of treason towards my country, and of an act of disloyalty towards the majesty of Heaven, which I revere above all earthly kings.

"Mr. President, it is natural to man to indulge in the illusions of Hope. We are apt to shut our eyes against a painful truth, and listen to the song of that siren, till she transforms us into beasts. Is this the part of wise men, engaged in a great and arduous struggle for liberty? Are we disposed to be of the number of those, who having eyes, see not, and having ears, hear not, the things which so nearly concern their temporal salvation? For my part, whatever anguish of spirit it may cost, I am willing to know the whole truth; to know the worst, and to provide for it.

"I have but one lamp by which my feet are guided; and that is the lamp of experience. I know of no way of judging of the future but by the past. And judging by the past, I wish to know what there has been in the conduct of the British ministry, for the last ten years, to justify those hopes with which gentlemen have been pleased to solace themselves and the House. Is it that insidious smile with which our petition has been lately received? Trust it not, Sir; it will prove a snare to your feet. Suffer not yourselves to be betrayed by a kiss. Ask yourselves how this gracious reception of our petition comports with those warlike preparations, which cover our waters and darken our land. Are fleets and armies necessary to a work of love and reconciliation? Have we shown ourselves so unwilling to be reconciled, that force must be called in to win back our love? Let us not deceive ourselves, Sir. These are the implements of war and subjugation; the last arguments to which kings resort. I ask gentlemen, Sir, what means this martial array, if its purpose be not to force us to submission? Can gentlemen assign any other possible motive for it? Has Great Britain any enemy in this quarter of the world, to call for all this accumulation of navies and armies? No, Sir, she has none. They are meant for us; they can be meant for no other. They are sent over to bind and rivet upon us those chains, which the British ministry have been so long forging. And what have we to oppose to them? Shall we try argument? Sir, we have been trying that for the last ten years. Have we anything new to offer upon the subject? Nothing. We have held the subject up in every light of which it is capable; but it has been all in vain. Shall we resort to entreaty and humble supplication? What terms shall we find, which have not been already exhausted? Let us not, I beseech you, Sir, deceive ourselves longer. Sir, we have done everything that could be done, to avert the storm which is now coming on. We have petitioned; we have remonstrated; we have supplicated; we have prostrated ourselves before the throne, and have implored its interposition to arrest the tyrannical hands of the Ministry and Parliament. Our petitions have been slighted; our remonstrances have produced additional violence and insult; our supplications have been disregarded; and we have been spurned, with contempt, from the foot of the throne. In vain, after these things, may we indulge the fond hope of peace and reconciliation. *There is no longer any room for hope.* If we wish to be free; if we mean to preserve inviolate those inestimable privileges for which we have been so long contending; if we mean not basely to abandon the noble struggle in which we have been so long engaged, and which we have pledged ourselves never to abandon, until the glorious object of our contest shall be obtained; we must fight! I repeat it, Sir, we must fight! An appeal to arms, and to the God of hosts, is all that is left us.

"They tell us, Sir, that we are weak; unable to cope with so formidable an adversary. But when shall we be stronger? Will it be the next week or the next year? Will it be when we are totally disarmed, and when a British guard shall be stationed in every house? Shall we gather strength by irresolution and inaction? Shall we acquire the means of effectual resistance by lying supinely on our backs, and hugging the delusive phantom of hope, until our enemies shall have bound us hand and foot? Sir, we are not weak, if we make a proper use of those means which the God of nature hath placed in our power. Three millions of people, armed in the holy cause of liberty, and in such a country as that which we possess, are invincible by any force which our enemy can send against us. Besides, Sir, we shall not fight our battles alone. There is a just God, who presides over the destinies of nations, and who will raise up friends to fight our battles for us. The battle, Sir, is not to the strong alone; it is to the vigilant, the active, the brave. Besides, Sir, we have no election. If we were base enough to desire it, it is now too late to retire from the contest. There is no retreat but in submission and slavery. Our chains are forged. Their clanking may be heard on the plains of Boston. The war is inevitable; and let it come! I repeat it, Sir, let it come!

"It is vain, Sir, to extenuate the matter. Gentlemen may cry, Peace, peace; but there is no peace. The war is actually begun. The next gale that sweeps from the north will bring to our ears the clash of resounding arms. Our brethren are already in the field. Why stand we here idle? What is it that gentlemen wish? What would they have? Is life so dear, or peace so sweet, as to be purchased at the price of chains and slavery? Forbid it, Almighty God! I know not what course others may take; but, as for me, give me liberty, or give me death!"

This spirited and powerful speech determined the character of the proceedings of the Convention. After another eloquent speech from Richard Henry Lee, in support of the resolutions, a committee, of which Henry and Washington were among the members, was appointed to prepare and report a plan for the organization of the militia. The report was accordingly made, and the plan adopted; after which, and the transaction of some other business of less importance, the Convention closed its session.

CHAPTER V.

Military Movements. — Henry appointed Commander-in-Chief of the Virginia Forces. — Resigns his Commission. — Elected the first Governor under the new Constitution.

Under the present system of conducting political and military affairs in the Christian world, it rarely happens that the same persons, whose opinions in council and eloquence in debate determine the commencement of hostile relations between two countries, are called upon themselves to share the personal hardships and dangers of the conflict. The political leaders, who direct the concerns of nations, content themselves, in general, with declaring wars, and leave it to others to carry them on. It has sometimes been thought that this division of labor has a tendency to render wars more frequent, and that statesmen would be less prompt in urging a resort to arms, if the blood which is to flow were to be their own. However this may be, it was pretty soon apparent that Patrick Henry was not one of those persons, who are disposed to shrink themselves from the dangers to which they may deem it necessary to expose their countrymen. We have thus far seen him engaged in the various civil employments of cultivator, merchant, lawyer, and statesman. At the next stage in his career, we find him assuming the character of a military leader, and discharging its duties with a spirit and efficiency which seem to show that, if circumstances of a wholly accidental nature had not checked his progress, his energies would probably have taken this direction, and given him as high a rank among the warriors of his country as he has in fact obtained among her orators and statesmen.

When the state of the controversy with the mother country began to render it probable, that it would be necessary to resort to arms, the Governors of the several colonies, either in consequence of instructions from home, or of a concert among themselves, attempted, at about the same time, to get possession of the military stores at all the various points at which they had been collected. On the 20th of April, 1775, the day following the celebrated 19th of April, which was distinguished by the attempt of Governor Gage, in Massachusetts, to seize the military stores at Cambridge and Concord in Massachusetts, a similar proceeding took place in Virginia under the direction of Lord Dunmore. About midnight, Captain Collins, of the armed schooner Magdalen, then lying at Burwell's Ferry, on James River, entered the city of Williamsburg, at the head of a body of marines, and carried away from the public magazine about twenty barrels of powder, which he succeeded in getting on board his schooner before day.

The next morning, when the transaction was made known, it created great excitement among the inhabitants, and a considerable number of them mustered in arms for the purpose of compelling Captain Collins to restore the powder. The members of the municipal government, with some difficulty, restrained this tumultuous movement; but afterwards, in their corporate capacity, addressed a memorial to Lord Dunmore on the subject. The Governor returned a verbal answer, in which he stated, that, having heard of an insurrection in a neighboring county, he had thought it necessary to remove the powder to a place of safety, but assured the petitioners, upon his word of honor, that, whenever it was wanted for any proper purpose, it should be delivered. This assurance, supported by the influence of Peyton Randolph, R. C. Nicholas, and other prominent and popular citizens, restored for a time the public tranquillity.

In the course of the following night, however, a false report was circulated that a body of marines had again landed from the Magdalen, at some distance from the city, for the purpose of plunder. The inhabitants again rose in arms,

and, by the intervention of the same eminent
patriots, were a second time persuaded to lay
them aside. The next day, when tranquillity
was entirely restored, the Governor sent a message
into the city by one of the magistrates, to
inform the people that, if they offered the least
violence to his secretary, Captain Foy, or to Captain
Collins, he would set the slaves at liberty,
and lay the town in ashes. This threat, issued
without any apparent necessity, since the two
officers whom it was intended to protect had
been quietly walking the streets without molestation
throughout the whole disturbance, increased
the irritation of the inhabitants, which
did not, however, at the moment, show itself in
any further act of open insurrection.

While the accounts of these proceedings were
rapidly circulating throughout the colony, intelligence
came on from the east of the events of the
19th of April at Lexington and Concord. The
effect was electrical. The volunteer companies,
which had recently been formed, for purposes
of discipline, under the direction of Lord Dunmore
himself, assembled in arms in every county.
By the 27th of April, seven hundred men, well
armed and disciplined, styling themselves friends
of constitutional liberty and America, were collected
at Fredericksburg, with the intention of
marching to the capital. This movement was

checked by an express, received from Peyton Randolph on the 29th of April, stating that the gentlemen of Williamsburg and its neighborhood were satisfied with the result of the seizure of the powder, and advised the volunteers to proceed no farther. On the receipt of this express, a council was held, consisting of a hundred and two persons, officers of companies, or delegates to the provincial Convention, who, after expressing in the strongest terms their opinion of the Governor's proceedings, and their readiness to march at a moment's warning, whenever it might be necessary, in defence of their rights and liberty, recommended to their comrades to return, for the present, to their homes. They also sent off messengers, with advices to the same effect, to other meetings of a similar kind, which had been called in several other parts of the colony.

In this way, the movement was checked for the moment in every county, excepting Hanover, where Henry had again fixed his residence. Far from sharing the solicitude that seems to have been felt by the prominent patriots of Williamsburg to suppress any violent ebullitions of popular feeling, he was rather disposed to encourage them, and avowed to his confidential friends that he considered the seizure of the powder as a fortunate occurrence. Convinced that hostilities were inevitable, he was pleased with any incident which naturally tended to awaken the military spirit of the colony, and induce the people to place themselves at once in a condition for effectual resistance. As soon as he received intelligence of the proceedings at Williamsburg, he immediately summoned the members of the volunteer company of Hanover county to meet him in arms at Newcastle, on the 2d of May, on business of urgent importance. He also called together the county committee at the same time and place.

At this meeting, after a powerful and eloquent address from Henry, on the topics appropriate to the occasion, it was decided to march at once to Williamsburg, and either recover the powder, or make reprisals to an equal amount upon the money in the public treasury. Captain Meredith, who commanded the volunteers, resigned his commission, and consented to serve as lieutenant under Henry, who was immediately elected captain, and without delay took up the line of march for Williamsburg. Ensign Goodall, in the mean time, was ordered to cross the country to King William county, which was the place of residence of the King's Receiver-General, Richard Corbin, and to obtain from him three hundred and thirty pounds, the estimated value of the powder, or to take him prisoner. The party reached the house of Mr. Corbin in the night, and surrounded it for the purpose of preventing his escape. The next morning, they were assured by the ladies of the family that the Receiver-General was not in the house; and, after satisfying themselves that the statement was correct, they left the place and rejoined Henry, agreeably to their orders, at Doncastle's ordinary, about sixteen miles above Williamsburg.

The movement of Henry created an intense excitement throughout the colony, and revived at once the military ardor which had been momentarily checked by the moderating influence of the patriots at Williamsburg. The volunteer companies rose again in all quarters, and marched across the country to join Henry. It is supposed that not less than five thousand men were on their way to meet him. The royalists were alarmed. The Governor immediately sent his family on board the Fowey man-of-war, which was lying in the harbor, and issued a proclamation, in which he denounced the movement as treasonable, and ordered the people to oppose and resist it. Even the prominent patriots inclined, as before, to a pacific course, and despatched several expresses in succession to Henry, for the purpose of persuading him to recede from his design, and disband his troops. Henry paid no attention to these remonstrances, but resolutely pursued his march, until, on arriving at Doncastle's ordinary, he was met by a messenger from the Governor, bringing him a bill of exchange, drawn by the Receiver-General, for the value of the powder.

In the mean time, the marines from the Fowey had been landed, and apprehensions were entertained by some that they would make reprisals, for the money thus extorted by Henry, upon the public treasury. Henry, in consequence, addressed a letter to Mr. Nicholas, the treasurer of the colony, in which he offered, if it should be thought necessary or expedient, to detach from his own troops a guard sufficient for the protection of the treasury. Nicholas declined the offer, and Henry returned with his volunteers to Hanover. Two days after, the Governor issued a proclamation, denouncing the conduct of "a certain Patrick Henry" as treasonable, and cautioning the people not to give him any aid or countenance. No attempt was, however, made to institute legal proceedings against him, or to give him any personal molestation. Immediately after his return, he proceeded to Philadelphia to take his seat in Congress. He was escorted by a numerous cavalcade of his neighbors as far as the Potomac, and was met at every stage on his route by addresses and other demonstrations of the public regard. No accounts are preserved of his action at this session of Congress; and a series of events occurred soon after in Virginia, which called for his service in another capacity, and withdrew him from the field of national politics, to which he never after returned.

About this time the conciliatory propositions of Lord North arrived, and the Governor convoked a meeting of the House of Burgesses. He appeared to consider the troubles as entirely at an end, and brought back his lady and family from their retreat on board the Fowey to his residence at Williamsburg. Scarcely, however, had this arrangement been carried into effect, when he took alarm again at some fresh demonstration of patriotic feeling which occurred in the city, and withdrew with his family to the sloop of war, from which he never returned. The House of Burgesses remonstrated strongly against this proceeding, but, finding the Governor resolute, they at length adjourned to the 12th of October having first acted on and rejected the proposals of the British ministry. Before the adjournment, they summoned a meeting of the Virginia Convention, which assembled at Richmond on the 24th of July.

The proceedings of this body, of which Henry was a member, were marked with great vigor and decision. Assuming that the Governor, by retiring from the capital and taking up his residence on board a ship of war, had virtually abdicated his authority, they constituted a Committee of Safety, to represent, in his absence, the executive branch of the government. An ordinance was also passed for a military organization of the colony, which provided, among other things, for raising two regiments of regular soldiers, to consist of one thousand and twenty privates, rank and file. The Convention next proceeded to elect officers for these regiments; and the choice they made shows, in a very striking manner, how strongly the public mind had been impressed by the vigor and efficiency of the late movement of Henry. Although till now wholly inexperienced in military affairs, he was appointed not only colonel of the first regiment, but commander-in-chief of all the forces raised, or to be raised, in Virginia. William Woodford, who had distinguished himself in the preceding war, was appointed colonel of the second regiment. Washington had already been appointed by Congress commander-in-chief of the continental army; and it does not appear that there was any other person in the colony, whose pretensions, on any other ground but that of mere seniority, could be supposed for a moment to outweigh the brilliant services of Henry, both civil and military.

It appears, however, from subsequent occurrences, that his appointment was not approved by the older patriots, who probably felt some jealousy of the rapid progress which he had already made in the political career, and some disgust at the freedom with which he had opposed their views on the most important subjects. The Committee of Safety, which constituted, for the time, the executive power of the colony, was composed of this class of persons, under the presidency of Edmund Pendleton, with whom Henry had been brought into collision at the second meeting of the Convention. The arrangement of this body was such as to render it necessary for Henry to resign his commission as colonel and commander-in-chief very shortly after his appointment, and before he had had an opportunity to exhibit the extent of his capacity for this department of the public service.

In consequence of the measures adopted by the Convention for the military organization of the colony, Lord Dunmore considered it as in a state of rebellion, and employed himself, with the naval and military forces under his command, in harassing the settlements on the coast. At the close of October, Captain Squire, of the British sloop of war Otter, threatened an attack on Hampton, in consequence of which the inhabitants sent to the Committee of Safety, at Williamsburg, for relief. Colonel Woodford, of the second regiment, was immediately despatched with a company of riflemen to take command of the troops. The attack was repulsed without much difficulty. Lord Dunmore next directed his attention to the county of Norfolk, where his movements became so distressing, that it appeared indispensable to check his career. Colonel Woodford was the person called upon by the Committee of Safety to perform this service. He was ordered to cross James River, at Sandy Point, with eight hundred men, and bring Lord Dunmore to action.

Henry had been desirous to be employed himself on this expedition, and had expressed his wishes to the Committee of Safety. As commander-in-chief, it would seem that he had a right to decide at what point his own presence would be most useful; but the committee, without regard to this consideration, had given the preference to Woodford. Henry's reasons for dissatisfaction did not end here. Colonel Woodford, after having been despatched on this expedition, considered himself as under the immediate direction of the Committee of Safety, or of the Convention, when in session, and made no communications whatever to Henry. On the 6th of December, Henry wrote him a letter, stating, in civil terms, that he had received no despatches from him for a long time, and requesting to be informed of his situation and proceedings. Woodford sent him the desired information, but remarked, at the same time, that, "when joined, he should always esteem himself immediately under the command of Henry, and would obey accordingly; but, when sent to command a separate and distinct body of troops, under the immediate instructions of the Committee of Safety, whenever that body, or the honorable Convention, were sitting, he should look upon it as his indispensable duty to address his intelligence to them, as the supreme power in the colony."

The question, having thus been brought to a direct issue between the two officers, was referred by Henry to the decision of the Committee of Safety. In the mean time, Woodford had obtained a brilliant victory over the British at the Great Bridge, which, by stamping his appointment with the seal of success, would naturally confirm the confidence of the committee in their own judgment, and their preference for Woodford over Henry. The correctness of Henry's view of the subject was, however, too apparent to be seriously questioned, and the committee, notwithstanding their partiality for Woodford, adopted the following order;

"In Committee, December, 1775. Resolved, unanimously, that Colonel Woodford, although acting upon a separate and detached command, ought to correspond with Colonel Henry, and make returns to him, at proper times, of the state and condition of the forces under his command; and also that he is subject to his orders, when the Convention or the Committee of Safety is not sitting; but that, whilst either of those bodies is sitting, he is to receive his orders from one of them."

The letter of the chairman of the committee, Mr. Pendleton, enclosing this order to Woodford, is given by Mr. Wirt, and exhibits not only partiality for Woodford, but a feeling of positive unkindness towards Henry. "Believe me, Sir," says Pendleton, "the unlucky step of calling that gentleman from our councils, where he was useful, into the field in an important station, the duties of which he must, in the nature of things, be an entire stranger to, has given me many an anxious and uneasy moment." And, again, "We shall not intermeddle with the appointment of a general officer by Congress, lest it should be thought propriety requires our calling, or rather recommending, our present first officer to that station." There is some plausibility in the former suggestion; but Mr. Pendleton well knew that genius, like that of Henry, supplies, under all circumstances, the want of mere routine. His recent campaign, at the head of the Hanover volunteers, had sufficiently shown his capacity for actual service in the field.

A new aspect was given to the position of

Henry as commander-in-chief, by the arrival of a corps of auxiliary troops, which had been requested from North Carolina, and which consisted of five or six hundred men, commanded by Colonel Howe. This officer, whose commission was prior in date to that of Woodford, was permitted by the latter to take command of all the forces. In this capacity he addressed his communications, as Woodford had done, to the Committee of Safety or the Convention, without regard to the rights of Henry as commander-in-chief, who thus found himself set aside, and, as it were, superseded, by an officer from another colony of only equal rank. The spirit which prompted these proceedings was displayed in a still more decisive form.

Six regiments had been raised by the Convention, in addition to the two commanded by Henry and Woodford; and an application was made to Congress to take the Virginia troops into continental pay. In acting on this subject, Congress consented to the request in favor of the six additional regiments only. This singular discrimination was, doubtless, the result of a suggestion from the Committee of Safety, made for the purpose of disgusting Henry, and of preventing him from being regarded by Congress as a candidate for one of the higher commissions. At this point the Convention interfered in support of the commander-in-chief of their election, and remonstrated vigorously against the proceedings of Congress, and requested that, if six regiments only could be taken into the continental service, the two that were first raised might be placed first on the list. Congress acceded to this request, but still gave way to the same malignant influence that had dictated the former arrangement, so far as to confer the appointment of brigadier-general, in the service of the United States, upon Colonels Howe and Lewis, offering Henry a commission of colonel. This he without hesitation declined, and at the same time resigned that which he held from the authorities of his own state.

The resignation of Henry created great discontent in the army, by whom he was regarded with enthusiastic admiration and attachment, as the most eminent patriot in the state. The troops immediately put on mourning, and proceeded in military array to his lodgings, where the officers presented to him the following address;

"*To Patrick Henry, Jun., Esq.* Deeply impressed with a grateful sense of the obligations we lie under to you, for the polite, humane, and tender treatment, manifested to us throughout the whole of your conduct, while we had the honor of being under your command, permit us to offer you our sincere thanks, as the only tribute we have in our power to pay to your real merits.

Notwithstanding your withdrawing yourself from the service fills us with the most poignant sorrow, as it at once deprives us of our father and general, yet, as gentlemen, we are compelled to applaud your spirited resentment to the most glaring indignity. May your merit shine as conspicuous to the world in general, as it hath done to us, and may Heaven shower its choicest blessings upon you."

To this address Henry returned the following answer;

"Gentlemen; I am exceedingly obliged to you for your approbation of my conduct. Your address does me the highest honor. This kind testimony of your regard for me would have been an ample reward for services much greater than those, which I have had the power to perform. I return you, and each of you, gentlemen, my best acknowledgments for the spirit, alacrity, and zeal, you have constantly shown in your several stations. I am unhappy to part with you. I leave the service, but I leave my heart with you. May God bless you, and give you success and safety, and make you the glorious instruments of saving our country."

After receiving this address from Henry, the officers invited him to dine with them at the Raleigh tavern, and were preparing, after dinner, to escort him out of town. In the mean time, the soldiers had assembled in a rather disorderly manner, and demanded their discharge, declaring that they would not consent to serve under any other commander than Henry. Perceiving that this movement, if not checked, might lead to serious consequences, Henry concluded to pass another night in town, during which he visited the troops at their barracks, and urged them to continue in the service, which, as he said, he had quitted for reasons interesting to himself alone. His exertions, backed by those of other favorite officers, proved successful, and the soldiers acquiesced without further difficulty in the new arrangement.

A feeling, similar to that which prevailed among the troops at Williamsburg, manifested itself, with equal distinctness, in other forms, and particularly in an address which was signed by more than ninety officers stationed at several different points, and, in part, under Colonel Woodford's immediate command.

In consequence of these demonstrations of opinion and feeling, in regard to the resignation of Henry, the Committee of Safety felt themselves obliged to publish a defence of their conduct, which appeared in a leading newspaper, with the signature of *A Friend of Truth*. The committee represent themselves as having, in the first instance, requested that all the state troops should be taken into the continental service, and that, when the Convention remonstrated against the discrimination made by Congress, the committee, in transmitting this remonstrance, had particularly urged a compliance with it, "as a point of great consequence to our harmony, in which may be involved the good of the common cause." The defence, being thus confined to a justification of the formal proceedings of the committee, has, of course, no tendency to repel the real charge, which is founded in the supposition of secret suggestions of an adverse character.

Such was the termination of the military career of Patrick Henry. There can, of course, be but one opinion, among men of correct feeling, in regard to the malignant intrigue by which it was brought about; but it may well be doubted whether the result was in any way really injurious, either to Henry or the country. His peculiar gift was eloquence, for which the military service would have afforded no field whatever; and, supposing even that he had exhibited, on trial, an aptitude for warlike affairs not inferior to his natural talent for public speaking, it may be questioned whether the army, at least in any other part than that of commander-in-chief, afforded as good a field for honorable and useful activity as the senate and the bar.

As the oracle of his native state, at the time beyond comparison the most prominent in the country, he occupied as important a place as could well have been secured by any other career of service. Had his age permitted him to take part in the debates of Congress, or to fill executive offices under the new constitution, he might have been rather more extensively known to his contemporaries at home and abroad; but, on the other hand, by having lived at a somewhat earlier period, and connected his name, as he did, with the first movements of the revolution, he obtained a very peculiar glory, with which hardly any other, growing out of the events of that time, can come into competition. The opposition which checked his military career, however unamiable and discreditable to those who were concerned in it, was perhaps not unnatural, considering the unceremonious manner in which he had resisted the advice and authority of the older political leaders. It was fortunate for him that the disgust and jealousy, which he thus provoked, produced no worse result than his forced retreat from the army, and a passing mortification, for which he was destined to receive very early and ample satisfaction from his grateful fellow-citizens.

The state of the relations between the colonies and the mother country virtually annulled the established forms of government, and it was necessary for the colonies to reorganize their political institutions on a new foundation. For this purpose, each colony was regarded as a distinct community, possessing, by the laws of nature, an inherent right, under existing circumstances, to adopt any form of government which it might prefer. The right was exercised through the agency of popular conventions; and a meeting of this kind was held at Williamsburg, in Virginia, on the 6th of May, 1776. Henry was elected a member of this body for the county of Hanover. On the 15th of May, Mr. Cary reported, from a committee of the whole House, with a suitable preamble, two important resolutions, one of which instructed the delegates to the General Congress to propose to that body a declaration of independence and a confederation of the colonies, while the other provided for raising a committee to prepare a declaration of rights, and a plan of government for the new commonwealth of Virginia.

In pursuance of the second resolution, a committee was appointed, consisting of thirty-four of the most prominent patriots, including Henry, and, among the others, Mr. Madison. On the 12th of June, the committee reported a declaration of rights, and, on the 29th, a plan of government, both which were unanimously adopted by the Convention. The declaration was prepared by

Jefferson, the constitution chiefly by George Mason, a neighbor and intimate friend of Washington. Jefferson had transmitted from Philadelphia, where he was then in attendance as a member in Congress, to his friend, Mr. Wythe, a plan of government, accompanied by a declaration of rights, to be submitted to the Convention. Before it was received, the plan of the committee had already been adopted; but it was subsequently modified, in some parts, in accordance with Mr. Jefferson's views, and the declaration which he had sent was prefixed to it as a preamble. This document coincides, in its general outline, and in many particular passages, with the Declaration of Independence, which was issued, on the 4th of July following, by the General Congress; and, as Mr. Jefferson's name was not at the time publicly connected with the Virginia Declaration, he has sometimes, on the strength of this coincidence, been accused of plagiarism in preparing that of the 4th of July. It is sufficient to say, in answer to this imputation, that the plan of government which he transmitted to Mr. Wythe, including the Declaration as it now stands in the statute-book, are still preserved, in Mr. Jefferson's hand-writing, in the archives of Virginia.

By the new constitution, the executive power was committed to a chief magistrate, with the title of governor, to be annually elected by the legislature, and to be eligible for three successive terms. For the purpose of putting the measure at once in operation, the Convention took upon themselves the responsibility of designating the chief magistrate, and thus obtained an opportunity of compensating Henry, by a signal mark of public favor, for the *glaring indignity* which, in the language of the address from the troops, had been offered him by the Committee of Safety. On proceeding to a choice, the votes stood as follows; Patrick Henry, sixty; Thomas Nelson, forty-five; John Page, one. Nelson had been president of the council, under the preceding government, and was probably put forward by the friends of the committee, as an opponent to Henry. He was afterwards elected a member of the new council, but declined the appointment on the score of age and infirmity.

In answer to the notice of his election, communicated to him by a committee of the Convention, the new Governor returned the following address;

" *To the Honorable the President and House of Convention.* Gentlemen; The vote of this day, appointing me Governor of the commonwealth, has been notified to me, in the most polite and obliging manner, by George Mason,

Henry Lee, Dudley Digges, John Blair, and Bartholomew Dandridge, Esquires.

"A sense of the high and unmerited honor conferred upon me by the Convention fills my heart with gratitude, which I trust my whole life will manifest. I take this earliest opportunity to express my thanks, which I wish to convey to you, gentlemen, in the strongest terms of acknowledgment.

"When I reflect that the tyranny of the British King and Parliament hath kindled a formidable war, now raging throughout this wide-extended continent, and in the operations of which this commonwealth must bear so great a part; and that, from the events of this war, the lasting happiness or misery of a great proportion of the human species will finally result; that, in order to preserve this commonwealth from anarchy, and its attendant ruin, and to give vigor to our councils, and effect to all our measures, government hath been necessarily assumed, and new-modelled; that it is exposed to numberless hazards, and perils, in its infantine state; that it can never attain to maturity, or ripen into firmness, unless it is guided by an affectionate assiduity, and managed by great abilities; I lament my want of talents; I feel my mind filled with anxiety and uneasiness, to find myself so unequal to the duties of that important station, to which I am called, by the favor of my fellow-citizens, at this truly critical conjuncture. The errors of my conduct shall be atoned for, so far as I am able, by unwearied endeavors to secure the freedom and happiness of our common country.

"I shall enter upon the duties of my office, whenever you, Gentlemen, shall be pleased to direct; relying upon the known wisdom and virtue of your honorable House to supply my defects, and to give permanency and success to that system of government which you have founded, and which is so wisely calculated to secure equal liberty, and advance human happiness.

"I have the honor to be, Gentlemen, your most obedient and very humble servant,

"P. Henry, Jun."

The election of Henry as Governor was received with great favor by the public, and especially by the troops. The two regiments, which he had recently commanded, presented to him the following address;

"May it please your Excellency; Permit us, with the sincerest sentiments of respect and joy, to congratulate your Excellency upon your unsolicited promotion to the highest honors a grateful people can bestow. Uninfluenced by private ambition, regardless of sordid interest, you have uniformly pursued the general good of your country; and have taught the world, that an ingenuous love of the rights of mankind, an inflexible resolution, and a steady perseverance in the practice of every public and private virtue, lead directly to preferment, and give the best title to the honors of our uncorrupted and vigorous state.

"Once happy under your military command, we hope for more extensive blessings from your civil administration.

"Intrusted as your Excellency is, in some measure, with the support of a young empire, our hearts are willing, and our arms ready, to maintain your authority as chief magistrate; happy that we have lived to see the day, when freedom and equal rights, established by the voice of the people, shall prevail through the land.

"We are, may it please your Excellency, your Excellency's most devoted and most obedient servants."

To this address Henry returned the following answer;

"Gentlemen of the First and Second Virginia Regiments; Your address does me the highest honor. Be pleased to accept my most cordial thanks for your favorable and kind sentiments of my principles and conduct.

"The high appointment to which my fellow-citizens have called me was, indeed, *unsolicited*, *unmerited.* I am, therefore, under increased obligations to promote the safety, dignity, and happiness of the commonwealth.

"While the civil powers are employed in establishing a system of government, liberal, equitable, in every part of which the genius of equal liberty breathes her blessed influence, to you is assigned the glorious task of saving, by your valor, all that is dear to mankind. Go on, Gentlemen, to finish the great work you have so nobly and successfully begun. Convince the tyrants again, that they shall bleed, that America will bleed to her last drop, ere their wicked schemes find success.

"The remembrance of my former connection with you shall be ever dear to me. I honor your profession, I revere that patriot virtue, which, in your conduct, hath produced cheerful obedience, exemplary courage, and contempt of hardship and danger. Be assured, Gentlemen, I shall feel the highest pleasure in embracing every opportunity to contribute to your happiness and welfare; and I trust the day will come, when I shall make one of those that will hail you among the triumphant deliverers of America.

"I have the honor to be, Gentlemen, your most obedient and very humble servant,

"P. Henry, Jun."

The Governor's palace at Williamsburg, which

had been previously converted into a hospital, was now restored to its original use; and, on the 5th of July, the new Governor and Council took the oaths of office, and entered on the discharge of their duties.

Thus had Henry, in the short space of thirteen years, which had elapsed since he argued the Parsons' Cause, on the 1st of December, 1763, ascended from the position of an obscure advocate and a mere private citizen, through the responsible stations of member of the Assembly, member of Congress, and commander-in-chief of the Virginia forces, to the chief magistracy of the commonwealth. He had risen solely by the effect of talent and character, without any aid from powerful connections, without the use of any courtly arts, without even the indefatigable and persevering industry, which sometimes supplies the absence of almost every other advantage. Jealousy and envy had tried their worst upon him, not without some transient success, but had signally failed in the end, in all their efforts to obstruct his progress and injure his position. The bar-keeper of the little inn at Hanover had become the occupant of the Governor's palace at Williamsburg. The "obscure advocate" of the Parsons' Cause was now the greatest orator in the country, and one of the leading statesmen and magistrates in a new political system, created in no small degree by his own exertions. The indolent youth, who, at five and twenty, seemed to have lost every chance for success and distinction, had assumed, before forty, an eminent position among those whom Bacon describes as the first class of great men, *the founders of nations.* The most difficult and important objects of his earthly mission were accomplished. We are now to follow him through the highly honorable but comparatively easy routine of political and professional duty, where we shall find him exhibiting the same talents and virtues which had carried him, with so much brilliancy and success, through the stormy struggles of the revolution.

CHAPTER VI.

Administration as Governor. — Return to private Life. — Reëlected Governor. — Resigns. — Elected to the Assembly.

The office of Governor of a state, however honorable as a mark of public esteem, is one, in general, of mere routine, and affords but little opportunity for the display of superior talents; especially in the line in which Henry was particularly distinguished, that of forensic and parliamentary eloquence. His term of service in this capacity is accordingly the portion of his life, which furnishes the most scanty supply of materials for the biographer. Soon after his entrance into office, Lord Dunmore evacuated the territory of the state. The military operations, which had been going on during the preceding year, were, in consequence, brought to a close, and were not renewed, to any considerable extent, while Henry was Governor. He had, therefore, no occasion for the exercise of the powers of commander-in-chief, which, as an appendage to the chief magistracy, had now been restored to him by the suffrages of the legislature. In his civil capacity his administration is represented as having been efficient and successful, but undistinguished by any event of extraordinary importance.

At the first session of the legislature after his election, an incident occurred of a singular, rather than very important, character, which seems to require some notice in an account of his life, although, from the means of information now extant and accessible, it is difficult to form a very satisfactory idea of it.

The Assembly met in the autumn of the year 1776, perhaps the most gloomy period of the war. The occupation of New York by the

British troops, and the losses sustained by Washington, in two or three actions in the neighborhood of that city, had, in a great measure, obliterated the recollection of the successes of the preceding year. The extreme difficulty of providing the resources necessary for keeping up even the appearance of opposition to the numerous well-disciplined and well-appointed armies of England began to be apparent. There was no assurance yet of any aid from abroad. Under these disastrous circumstances, a vague imagination seems to have crossed the minds of a portion of the members of the Virginia legislature, that something might be gained by a recourse to the expedient so often adopted by the Romans in cases of great emergency, the concentration of the whole civil and military power of the republic in the hands of a single person, with the title of dictator.

The inutility, in reference to the general situation of the country, of constituting a state dictator, who would have had, as such, no right to exercise his unbounded powers out of the narrow limits of his own dominion, or for any other than state objects, was sufficiently obvious, one would have thought, to satisfy the least judicious person that such a project, if not dangerous, was wholly destitute of plausibility. It is certain, however, that the plan was contemplated, for it became the subject of warm and acrimonious discussion among the members of the Assembly. It is also known that Henry was the person, whom the projectors of this scheme intended to create dictator. There is no proof that he had himself any share in the plan, which was even distinctly disavowed at the time, and ever since, by himself and his friends. It appears, however, that he did not escape suspicion. While the project was in agitation, Colonel Archibald Cary, then speaker of the Assembly, a patriot of great consideration, but of a somewhat violent temper, met, in the lobby of the house, Colonel Syme, the brother-in-law of Henry, and addressed him as follows; "I am told, that your brother wishes to be dictator; tell him, from me, that the day of his appointment shall be the day of his death; for he shall feel my dagger in his heart before the sunset of that day." Colonel Syme replied, in great agitation, that, if such a project existed, his brother would certainly never lend himself to it, or to any other plan which would endanger the liberty of the country.

Whatever apprehensions may have been entertained at the time by individuals, it is certain that no unfavorable impression was produced upon the general feeling of the Assembly, for, at the next annual election, on the 30th of May, 1777, Henry was unanimously reëlected Governor, the members of the legislature being mostly the same as those of the preceding year, and Colonel Cary being again the presiding officer of the House. It does not appear from the account, that the project was at this time formally proposed to the Assembly; but four years afterwards, at another period of general alarm, when the territory of Virginia had become again the theatre of actual hostilities, and when the session of the legislature had been interrupted by an inroad of British troops, the project was again started, and not only made the subject of consideration in private, but actually proposed in the Assembly, and lost by only a very few votes.

Mr. Jefferson, who was then Governor of the state, and had, of course, the strongest motives for informing himself, as far as possible, of the real character of this singular scheme, denounces it, in strong terms, in his Notes on Virginia, but acquits the persons implicated in it, whom he does not name, of anything worse than an error of judgment. Henry was now, as before, the intended dictator; and, as the plan must have been within his knowledge, it seems hardly possible that it could have been entertained for years in succession, and finally proposed in the legislature, without his concurrence. Supposing that he suggested or favored it, there is, of course, no reason to suspect that he had any other object in view than the ostensible one of the public good.

His favorite reading was the history of Rome; and the example of that illustrious commonwealth, as well as his own experience, had shown him the entire incapacity of deliberative assemblies for the conduct of military affairs. The real objection to the plan of a state dictator was not, in fact, the danger resulting from the existence of such an office to the public liberty, but its utter inefficiency for the defence of the Union. The expediency of something of the kind, for state purposes, was felt in Virginia, in 1781; and, although the plan of creating a dictator was rejected, resolutions were passed, conferring on the Governor and Council extraordinary powers, amounting to an unlimited control over the purse and sword of the state, and requesting Congress to intrust authority of a similar description to the commander-in-chief of the forces of the Union, which was, in fact, done. The concern, if any, which Henry may have had in the project of constituting a dictator need not, therefore, diminish our confidence in his patriotism, although it might, perhaps, impair, in some degree, our respect for his judgment. Even in this particular, as the tendency of his mind was always for the boldest and most energetic course of action, the plan would not have been very much at variance with the predominant traits of his character.

During the second year of Henry's administration as Governor occurred the intrigue against the influence of Washington, which has sometimes been called the *Conway Cabal*. The origin, character, extent, and precise objects, of this conspiracy are not very exactly known. It appears to have included a good many members of Congress, and some distinguished officers of the army. The success of General Gates, in the capture of the British troops under Burgoyne, seems to have given to Gates himself, and perhaps to others, the impression that he was superior, in efficiency as a commander, to Washington. Those who held this opinion may have thought it politic and patriotic to endeavor to substitute Gates for Washington in the chief command. Other influences, of a less honorable kind, no doubt, had their effect in determining the movement. The existence of the intrigue was made known to Washington through the indiscretion of General Conway, and the odium of the affair has finally rested upon him more directly than upon any other person, though it is difficult to view him in any other light than as an instrument of Gates. The intention seems to have been to act through the medium of

Congress, where the cabal had supporters; to disgust Washington by repeated slights, until he should be induced to resign, and then to appoint Gates in his place.

The appointment of Conway to the place of Inspector-General of the army, against the express advice of Washington, and after his hostility to the commander-in-chief was known, was the strongest demonstration made by the conspirators towards carrying their views into effect. The discovery of the plot by Washington, and his cool and discreet, but at the same time firm, conduct on the occasion, apparently disconcerted the leaders, and checked their operations for the time; while the total failure of Gates, in his southern campaign, removed every honest and plausible pretext for a change. Conway's characteristic indiscretion afterwards involved him in a controversy with Congress, which led to his compulsory resignation, and in a duel which nearly cost him his life. While suffering from the effect of his wounds, and in expectation of immediate dissolution, he wrote a penitential letter to Washington, in which he avows, with expressions of deep regret, his share in the plot, and declares Washington to be, in his eyes, the "great and good man." This voluntary confession of the principal agent in the plot, while it does but little to atone for his guilt, is valuable as a complete bar to the suspicion, which might otherwise have arisen in some minds, that there was a real foundation for imputations of some sort upon the character or capacity of Washington. An attempt was made to implicate Henry in this cabal. An anonymous letter was sent to him, on this subject, dated at Yorktown, January 12th, 1778.

A passage in that letter, which is given as an extract from a letter of General Conway to a friend, coincides exactly in substance, and very nearly in the language, with one in a letter from Conway to Gates, which accidentally became known to Washington, and first revealed to him the existence of the plot. It is worthy of remark, that the substantial genuineness of the latter passage is here avowed by one of the conspirators, although the defence afterwards set up by Gates, when the affair was brought home to him by Washington, was, that the supposed extract was not in the letter, and was a "wicked forgery." The true state of the case might easily have been shown by producing the letter, which the conspirators never ventured to do. The reality of the passage in question is admitted by the strongest implication, in the first letters, written by Conway and Gates to Washington on the subject, as was remarked by Washington at the time, in his pointed and manly reply to the latter. It is here directly avowed by one of the conspirators. The pretence of forgery was evidently an after-thought. This overture was treated by Henry in the way which might have been expected from his known character. He transmitted the communication to Washington, enclosed in the following letter;

"*Williamsburg, February* 20*th*, 1778. Dear Sir; You will, no doubt, be surprised at seeing the enclosed letter, in which the encomiums bestowed on me are as undeserved, as the censures aimed at you are unjust. I am sorry there should be one man who counts himself my friend, who is not yours.

"Perhaps I give you needless trouble in handing you this paper. The writer of it may be too insignificant to deserve any notice. If I knew this to be the case, I should not have intruded on your time, which is so precious. But there may possibly be some scheme or party forming to your prejudice. The enclosed leads to such a suspicion. Believe me, Sir, I have too high a sense of the obligations America has to you, to abet or countenance so unworthy a proceeding. The most exalted merit hath ever been found to attract envy. But I please myself with the hope, that the same fortitude and greatness of mind, which have hitherto braved all the difficulties and dangers inseparable from your station, will rise superior to every attempt of the envious partisan.

"I really cannot tell who is the writer of this letter, which not a little perplexes me. The hand-writing is altogether strange to me.

"To give you the trouble of this gives me pain. It would suit my inclination better to give you some assistance in the great business of the war. But I will not conceal anything from you by which you may be affected; for I really think your personal welfare and the happiness of America are intimately connected. I beg you will be assured of that high regard and esteem, with which I ever am, dear Sir, your affectionate friend and very humble servant."

On the 5th of March, Henry wrote a second letter to Washington on the same subject, as follows;

"Dear Sir; By an express which Colonel Finnie sent to camp, I enclosed to you an anonymous letter, which I hope got safe to hand. I am anxious to hear something that will serve to explain the strange affair, which I am now informed is taken up respecting you. Mr. Custis has just paid us a visit, and by him I learn sundry particulars concerning General Mifflin, that much surprised me. It is very hard to trace the schemes and windings of the enemies to America. I really thought that man its friend; however, I am too far from him to judge of his present temper.

"While you face the armed enemies of our liberty in the field, and, by the favor of God, have been kept unhurt, I trust your country will never harbor in her bosom the miscreant who would ruin her best supporter. I wish not to flatter; but when arts, unworthy honest men, are used to defame and traduce you, I think it not amiss, but a duty, to assure you of that estimation in which the public hold you. Not that I think any testimony I can bear is necessary for your support, or private satisfaction; for a bare recollection of what is past must give you sufficient pleasure in every circumstance of life. But I cannot help assuring you, on this occasion, of the high sense of gratitude which all ranks of men in this your native country bear to you. It will give me sincere pleasure to manifest my regards, and render my best services to you or yours. I do not like to make a parade of these things, and I know you are not fond of it; however, I hope the occasion will plead my excuse.

"Wishing you all possible felicity, I am, my dear Sir, your ever affectionate friend, and very humble servant." *

In the spring of 1778, Henry was unanimously

---

* Washington's answers, and all the letters on this subject, may be found in WASHINGTON's WRITINGS, Vol. V. pp. 483-518.

reëlected Governor. At the close of the year, although he had served three terms, and was consequently no longer eligible by the constitution, it seems to have been the wish and intention of some of the members of the legislature to reëlect him once more, on the ground, that, as he was chosen the first time by the Convention, and not by the legislature, the period during which he was constitutionally eligible did not commence till the second year of his administration. Henry, however, did not think proper to acquiesce in this construction of the constitution, and declined a reëlection in the following letter to the speaker of the Assembly;

"*May 28th*, 1779. Sir; The term for which I had the honor to be elected Governor by the late Assembly being just about to expire, and the constitution, as I think, making me ineligible to that office, I take the liberty to communicate to the Assembly, through you, Sir, my intention to retire in four or five days.

"I have thought it necessary to give this notification of my design, in order that the Assembly may have the earliest opportunity of deliberating upon the choice of a successor to me in office.

"With great regard, I have the honor to be, Sir, your most obedient servant."

In the autumn of 1784, six years after the close of his former term of service, Henry, being now eligible by the constitution, was again elected Governor, and, at the termination of his official year, was reëlected to the same office. It was the wish and intention of the legislature, that he should have completed another three years' term; but, at the end of the second year, he declined a reëlection.

The motive which induced him to decline was the embarrassed state of his private affairs. Although his manner of living was entirely free from ostentation, he had found the salary allowed him as Governor insufficient to cover his expenses, and had been compelled to contract debts which he had no means of paying, but by the sale of a part of his estate, or by resuming the practice of his profession. He judiciously chose the latter course. During his employment in the public service, some changes had taken place in his private relations. His wife, after lingering through several years of ill-health and suffering, had died. Soon after this event, he had sold the estate on which he had been residing in Hanover county, and had purchased a tract of eight or ten thousand acres of land in the new county of Henry, which had been erected during his administration, and called by his name.

In the year 1777, he espoused, in second nuptials, a daughter of Mr. A. W. Dandridge, and fixed his residence at his newly-acquired estate, called Leatherwood. On resuming his attendance in the courts, he confined himself chiefly to the duties of counsellor and advocate, leaving it to his junior associates to attend to technical details. He was employed in all the cases of importance, as well in other parts of the state, as in his own immediate neighborhood. After the close of his first term of service as Governor, he was elected a member of the Assembly, and continued till the close of his active life to take a prominent part in the proceedings of that body. In this field of action he distinguished himself by liberality of feeling and soundness of judgment, not less than by the superiority of his powers in debate.

Immediately after the close of the revolution, he proposed in the Assembly, that the persons who had left the state, in consequence of their adherence to the policy of the mother country, should be permitted to return. This measure was violently resisted, but was finally adopted, chiefly under the impression produced by his overwhelming eloquence. A report of his speech on this occasion has been preserved, and is remarkable for its correct views of the economical situation of the country, and its sagacious foresight of the future course of events, as well as for its noble sentiments and richness of language. Judge Tyler, then speaker of the Assembly, opposed the measure with extreme violence in the committee of the whole, and, appealing personally to Henry, as one of its principal supporters, expressed his wonder, that he, of all men, after standing forward as the great champion of independence, should now appear as the advocate of the detested refugees. Henry replied as follows.

"The personal feelings of a politician ought not to be permitted to enter these walls. The question is a national one, and, in deciding it, if we act wisely, nothing will be regarded but the interest of the nation. On the altar of my country's good I am willing to sacrifice all personal resentments, all private wrongs; and I flatter myself, that I am not the only man in the House who is capable of making such a sacrifice. We have, Sir, an extensive country, *without population*; what can be a more obvious policy than that this country ought to be peopled? *People*, Sir, form the strength, and constitute the wealth, of a nation. I want to see our vast forests filled up by some process a little more speedy than the ordinary course of nature. I wish to see these states rapidly ascending to that rank which their natural advantages authorize them to hold among the nations of the earth.

"Cast your eyes, Sir, over this extensive country; observe the salubrity of your climate; the variety and fertility of your soil; and see that soil intersected in every quarter by bold, navigable streams, flowing to the east and to the west, as if the finger of Heaven were marking out the course of your settlements, inviting you to enterprise, and pointing the way to wealth. Sir, you are destined, at some time or other, to become a great agricultural and commercial people; the only question is, whether you choose to reach this point by slow gradations, and at some distant period; lingering on through a long and sickly minority; subjected, meanwhile, to the machinations, insults, and oppressions, of enemies, foreign and domestic, without sufficient strength to resist and chastise them; or whether you choose rather to rush at once, as it were, to the full enjoyment of those high destinies, and be able to cope, single-handed, with the proudest oppressor of the old world. If you prefer the latter course, as I trust you do, encourage emigration; encourage the husbandmen, the mechanics, the merchants, of the old world, to come and settle in this land of promise; make it the home of the skilful, the industrious, the fortunate, and happy, as well as the asylum of the distressed; fill up the measure of your population as speedily as you can, by the means which Heaven hath placed in your power; and I venture to prophesy there are those now living, who will see this favored land amongst the most powerful on earth; able,

Sir, to take care of herself, without resorting to that policy which is always so dangerous, though sometimes unavoidable, of calling in foreign aid. Yes, Sir; they will see her great in arts and in arms; her golden harvests waving over fields of immeasurable extent; her commerce penetrating the most distant seas, and her cannon silencing the vain boasts of those who now proudly affect to rule the waves.

"But, Sir, you must have *men*; you cannot get along without them; those heavy forests of valuable timber, under which your lands are groaning, must be cleared away; those vast riches which cover the face of your soil, as well as those which lie hid in its bosom, are to be developed and gathered only by the skill and enterprise of men; your timber, Sir, must be worked up into ships, to transport the productions of the soil from which it has been cleared; then you must have commercial men and commercial capital to take off your productions, and find the best markets for them abroad. Your great want, Sir, is the want of *men*, and these you must have, and will have speedily, if you are wise.

"Do you ask how you are to get them? Open your doors, Sir, and they will come in; the population of the old world is full to overflowing; that population is ground, too, by the oppressions of the governments under which they live. Sir, they are already standing on tiptoe upon their native shores, and looking to your coasts with a wishful and longing eye; they see here a land blessed with natural and political advantages which are not equalled by those of any other country upon earth; a land on which a gracious Providence hath emptied the horn of abundance; a land over which Peace hath now stretched forth her white wings, and where content and plenty lie down at every door! Sir, they see something still more attractive than all this; they see a land in which Liberty hath taken up her abode; that Liberty, whom they had considered as a fabled goddess, existing only in the fancies of poets; they see her here a real divinity, her altars rising on every hand throughout these happy states, her glories chanted by three millions of tongues, and the whole region smiling under her blessed influence. Sir, let but this our celestial goddess, Liberty, stretch forth her fair hand toward the people of the old world, tell them to come, and bid them welcome, and you will see them pouring in from the north, from the south, from the east, and from the west; your wildernesses will be cleared and settled, your deserts will smile, your ranks will be filled, and you will soon be in a condition to defy the powers of any adversary.

"But gentlemen object to any accession from Great Britain, and particularly to the return of the British refugees. Sir, I feel no objection to the return of those deluded people; they have, to be sure, mistaken their own interests most wofully, and most wofully have they suffered the punishment due to their offences. But the relations which we bear to them and to their native country are now changed; their king hath acknowledged our independence; the quarrel is over; peace hath returned, and found us a free people. Let us have the magnanimity, Sir, to lay aside our antipathies and prejudices, and consider the subject in a political light. Those are an enterprising, moneyed people; they will be serviceable in taking off the surplus produce of our lands, and supplying us with necessaries during the infant state of our manufactures. Even if they be inimical to us in point of feeling and principle, I can see no objection, in a political view, to making them tributary to our advantage. And as I have no prejudices to prevent my making this use of them, so, Sir, I have no fear of any mischief that they can do us. Afraid of *them!* What, Sir, shall *we*, who have laid the proud British *lion* at our feet, now be afraid of his *whelps?*"

The concluding phrase is not, perhaps, entitled, as a specimen of rhetoric, to all the praise that has been bestowed upon it; but it is impossible to speak too favorably of the substance of the speech. The liberality of our institutions, and especially the generous and truly wise policy which throws open our vacant territory, at a merely nominal price, to all who choose to occupy it, are working out the results predicted by Henry with a rapidity, which even his ardent imagination could hardly have anticipated.

In the same liberal spirit, he supported and carried, against a vigorous opposition, a proposal for removing the restraints on British commerce. It was apprehended by some, that a free admission of British ships would exclude the trade of all other nations, and deprive us of the advantage of competition in reducing the price of our supplies from abroad. Henry repelled this objection with splendid eloquence; enlarged on the distress which the people had suffered by the interruption of foreign commerce; and concluded with proclaiming, in emphatic language, the doctrine of the liberty of trade, less familiar to the public ear at that time than it is now. "Why should we fetter commerce?" was his concluding remark; "a man in chains droops and bows to the earth; his spirits are broken; but let him twist the fetters from his legs, and he will stand upright. Fetter not Commerce, Sir; let her be as free as air. She will range the whole creation, and return on the wings of the four winds of heaven to bless the land with plenty."

During the session of 1784, Henry proposed in the Assembly a measure marked by the same originality of thought, and humanity of feeling, which dictated the others, but somewhat questionable, perhaps, on the score of practicability and expediency. The inconvenience which had been suffered, during the last and preceding wars, from the aggressions of the neighboring Indians, appeared to render it a matter of high importance to inspire them in some way with more amicable sentiments. Formal treaties of peace and alliance were known to be wholly ineffectual. Henry proposed to effect the object by a law to encourage intermarriage between the two races, and brought in a bill holding out strong inducements to the formation of connections of this kind, such as a pecuniary bounty, to be repeated at the birth of every child, exemption from taxes, and the free use of an institution for education, to be established for the purpose at the expense of the state.

The bill had its first and second reading, and was engrossed for its final passage, apparently under the influence of Henry's support; for no sooner was he withdrawn from the House, by his election as Governor for a second term, which took place at this time, than the bill, on coming up for a third reading, was rejected. Had the relative numbers and positions of the two races been

destined to remain as they were at this time, such
a measure might have had a good effect, although the popular feeling, which has always
been opposed to a mixture of races, would have
probably rendered it ineffectual. But the overwhelming and constantly increasing preponderance of the whites, in power and numbers, pretty
soon settled the question in a different way, by
compelling the red men to retire from the frontiers of Virginia, and seek for new hunting
grounds in the far west.

Among the measures supported, though not
proposed, by Henry, was a resolution for the incorporation of all Christian societies which might
make application to that effect, and another imposing a general assessment for the support of
public worship, but leaving it to the discretion
of the individual to appropriate the tax levied
upon him to any church which he might prefer.
The bills founded upon these resolutions were
reported after Henry had ceased to be a member
of the House; but the principles imbodied in
them had received his warm support in the introductory stage. The bill founded on the first
of the two resolutions became a law; the other
was rejected by a small majority, on the third
reading.

On the 4th of December, 1786, soon after his
final retirement from the chief magistracy of his

state, Henry was elected by the legislature one
of the delegates to the Convention for revising
the Articles of Confederation among the states.
His name stood upon the list, as recorded in the
journal, next after that of Washington. The
same imperious consideration, which had compelled him to decline reëlection as Governor, the
urgent necessity of attending to his private affairs, also imposed it upon him as a duty to
refrain from the acceptance of this high and
honorable commission, the full importance of
which was not, however, so distinctly perceived
at the time as it is now. After the national
Convention, which met the following year at
Philadelphia, had terminated their labors, and
submitted the result to the people, a state Convention was called in Virginia, to take the proposed constitution into consideration. Henry
was elected by the county of Prince Edward,
where he then resided, a member of this body,
which met at Richmond on the 2d of June,
1788.

CHAPTER VII.

Virginia Convention for considering the Plan of the Federal Constitution. — Henry opposes its Adoption.

In following the progress of Henry through his long political career up to the point which we have now reached, we have more than once seen him acting upon his own views, in direct opposition to those of the most distinguished and patriotic of his fellow-laborers, in the common cause of independence and liberty. On all these occasions he had the satisfaction of finding his course sanctioned, after a short interval, by the almost unanimous approbation of his fellow-citizens; and the public opinion of the country seems to have settled down in the conviction that the bold, vigorous, and, as it may have appeared to some at the time, violent policy, which he recommended and acted on, was the one best fitted to effect the common purpose.

In regard to the course which he pursued in the Convention for considering the plan of the federal constitution, he did not enjoy the same good fortune. He appeared in that Assembly as a determined opponent of the adoption of the plan, and maintained his views throughout the whole discussion with his characteristic ardor, perseverance, and power of logic and eloquence. Taking the whole country through, he was by far the most distinguished and conspicuous person, who opposed the new system. The great prosperity which the country has enjoyed for half a century in succession under this system, and which is justly attributed in no small degree to its beneficial influence, has long since stamped the constitution with the seal of general favor. It is now a matter of surprise and regret, to find that any one, and especially one so renowned as Henry for talent, patriotism, and eloquence, should have failed to perceive what has since become so apparent to all, and should have labored with so much earnestness to prevent the adoption of a system that has proved, in practice, the salvation of the country. We are half tempted to doubt, whether the opponents of the constitution acted with correct intentions and purely patriotic feelings, in resisting a measure which appears to us, at the present day, so clearly and manifestly right, and to attribute their course to perversity and selfishness, rather than to the lofty and patriotic motives upon which it was at the time justified by themselves.

We must recollect, however, in forming an opinion upon their conduct, that the constitution presented itself to their minds under a very different aspect from that in which it now appears to us. It came before the State Conventions, no doubt, under circumstances, in some respects, of the most auspicious character. It was offered as the result of the long and anxious deliberations of a most respectable assembly; it bore the signature of Washington. But there were other considerations connected with it of a different kind. It was known that the Convention had been greatly divided in opinion, and that the most important provisions in the constitution had been sanctioned by the smallest possible majorities, after the most intense and bitter opposition. The plan was untried, and patriotism imperiously required that an untried system, involving a complete revolution in the government, should be examined with extreme jealousy. This appeared the more necessary, as the Convention, in framing a new government, instead of merely amending the existing one, had in some degree exceeded its formal powers.

The system presented, in its most conspicuous, if not most important, features, particularly that of a single executive magistrate, forms repugnant to the cherished and habitual feelings of the people. These feelings were, of course, not diminished, in the present instance, by the knowledge, that the prominent friends of the constitution had urged, with great earnestness, in the Convention, the adoption of the provisions in a much more obnoxious shape. If the tendency of the system, as it stood, were considered doubtful, the fact that its ablest supporters in the Convention declared the British constitution, especially in the executive branch, to be the model of a good government, might well justify the suspicion that the new project had, as Henry remarked, an "awful squinting towards monarchy." It may even be doubted, whether the views of the opponents of the plan were not, on some points, more correct than those of its supporters, and whether the immense amount of good, which has resulted from the adoption of the constitution, may not have been the effect of its great leading principles, operating in spite, rather than by the aid, of some provisions, which were considered at the time, both by friends and opponents, as more important than they really were, and which, so far as they have operated, have been of injurious rather than beneficial tendency. On the whole, it not only seems unnecessary to attribute the action of the opponents of the constitution to perversity or selfish views, but it may even be doubted whether the course pursued by them was not the one, which would most naturally recommend itself to an ardent and uncompromising friend of popular principles of government.

The point upon which the debates in the General Convention chiefly turned was the question, whether the states should possess an equal vote in Congress, as had been the case under the old confederacy, or a number of votes proportional in each case to their comparative population. The Virginia plan, as it was called, which had been proposed by Governor Randolph, was supported with great power by Mr. Madison, who recommended the latter course. The former was the leading feature in the New Jersey plan, proposed by Mr. Paterson. After protracted and warm debates, the point was finally compromised by granting to the states an equal vote in the Senate, and a proportional one in the House of Representatives. This arrangement was not satisfactory, at the time, to the ardent supporters of either principle.

Some of the most prominent champions of the New Jersey scheme actually quitted the Convention and returned home, after it was agreed upon, under the impression that the rights of the states had been abandoned, that the compromise could never be sanctioned by them, and that there could be no advantage in taking any further part in the proceedings. On the other hand, the most active friends of the Virginia model were equally dissatisfied, though for a directly opposite reason. Governor Randolph refused to affix his name to his own plan as amended, and Mr. Madison, its principal champion, although he consented to sign it, declared, and has recorded the opinion in his report of the debates, that he considered it as completely vitiated by the introduction of the equal vote of the states in the Senate, which would, as he thought, inevitably perpetuate in the new system the essential vices of the old confederacy.

But, though the prominent supporters of the Virginia scheme in the Convention were wholly discontented with the result, they were generally considered, by the people at large of all parties, as having substantially carried their point, and given to the general government a great increase of strength, as compared with that which it possessed under the confederacy. The experience of half a century has confirmed the correctness of this view of the subject. The equal vote of the states in the Senate has not thus far proved to be of any practical importance for the purpose which led to its introduction. All the struggles that have taken place in Congress, including even those in which the respective pretensions of the states and the general government were directly at issue, have been decided by comparison of the strength of great parties pervading the whole Union, as represented in both branches of Congress, and not by the votes of the states, as represented on a footing of equality in the Senate;

while the whole history of the country, before and since the adoption of the constitution, proves, beyond a shadow of doubt, that the power of the general government, under the present system, is much greater than it was under the confederacy. The difference is, in fact, nearly equivalent to that between a government sufficiently powerful for every desirable purpose, and no government at all.

In accordance with the impression which prevailed at the time, and has thus been confirmed by experience, respecting the substantial character of the plan proposed by the Convention, it received, in general, when submitted to the people, the support of those who favored the Virginia system, and the idea of strengthening the general government. Even the prominent champions of the Virginia scheme in the Convention, who had so strongly expressed their dissatisfaction with it as amended by that body, seem, on full consideration, to have taken a more favorable view of the result. Governor Randolph, who had refused to sign the plan as adopted, and Mr. Madison, who declared that he considered the original Virginia scheme as entirely vitiated by the amendments, were the two most active and prominent supporters of the constitution in the Virginia Convention. Even Hamilton, who had said, in the Federal Convention, that he thought both the plans proposed entirely worthless from their inefficiency, and regarded the British constitution as the model of a good government, appeared in the New York State Convention as the leading champion of the plan, and labored, through the press, with his characteristic talent and energy, in concurrence with Madison and Jay, in recommending it to the people. On the other hand, the opposition to the plan in the State Conventions was generally led by the members of the General Convention, who had sustained in that body the pretensions of the states, and looked with apprehension to any decided augmentation of the power of the Union.

Patrick Henry, as was stated in the last chapter, had been appointed a delegate from Virginia to the General Convention, but, from prudential motives, had declined to accept the trust. He was, therefore, not personally committed to either of the parties which had been formed in that body; but there were several circumstances in his character and position, which naturally led him to sympathize in opinion and feeling with the partisans of the states. His native commonwealth was, at that time, by far the most important member of the Union. Any increase of the power of the general government, as compared with that of the states, operated, of course, more directly upon Virginia than upon any of her sisters. While several of the prominent Virginia statesmen, such as Washington, Madison, Randolph, Marshall, and others, overcame, by considerations of a more general character, the force of this local feeling, it was not unnatural that others, and especially those whose political career had identified their personal importance very closely with that of their own state, should look at the whole question chiefly in reference to the manner in which it affected state interests, and, finding its operation in this respect unfavorable to Virginia, should, for this reason only, decide against it.

This was preëminently the case with Henry. He had been, through the most active period of his life, the most prominent citizen in the Old Dominion, had occupied her highest places of trust and honor, both civil and military, and had imparted to them, by his splendid eloquence, a consideration, which, as mere official employments, they would not otherwise have had. On the other hand, he had taken little or no part in the administration of the general government; had not particularly distinguished himself as a member of Congress, and had no reason to consider his personal importance or reputation as immediately involved in the turn that might be taken by the affairs of the Union.

It may be added, that, while he was thus naturally led, by his personal associations and previous career, to favor the importance of the states, rather than that of the general government, he was also strongly disposed, by his peculiar views, to look with disapprobation upon any attempt to enlarge, in any way, the attributes of government, whether state or general, at the expense of the rights of the people. He had professed, and acted on, through life, very often under difficult circumstances, and with painful sacrifices of personal comfort, the most decidedly republican principles of government, had constituted himself, in his own state, a sort of tribune of the people, and protector of their rights against the influence of a wealthy aristocracy, and was probably the most determined republican, as well as the most zealous state rights man, in the country. There was, therefore, in his case, a remarkable concurrence of all the circumstances, that could well be expected to operate in producing in the mind of any individual a disposition, independently of the actual merits of the case, to oppose the new plan. Those who reflect upon the immense influence of accidental circumstances on the will and judgment, who recollect how large a portion of their own opinions, on the most important subjects, have been mainly determined by causes substantially of this character, will not be surprised, however strong their conviction may be of the essential excellence of the federal constitution, that a patriot so pure, intelligent, and sagacious, as Henry, should have been found, at the time of its adoption, among its most active opponents.

It is, therefore, unnecessary to suppose, as some have done, that Henry, and the other prominent opponents of the constitution, were actuated by personal or selfish motives. We may even go farther, and admit that there was not only great plausibility, but much actual truth, in some of their views. However beneficial may have been the operation of the federal constitution as a whole, it is not to be disguised, that, under some of its aspects, its tendency is different. This remark is made with particular allusion to the provision for the chief executive magistracy, which may, perhaps, be considered, with propriety, as the weak point in the constitution.

Our governments, both state and national, viewed under one of these aspects, belong to the class of elective monarchies; and, although the shortness of the term for which our rulers are elected, and the limited extent of the powers intrusted to them, abate very much the agitation naturally incident to this form of polity, experience has already shown that the difficulty is by no means entirely overcome. By throwing into the lottery of political life the glittering prize of the presidency, we have greatly augmented the intensity and eagerness of the struggle for official distinction. If the constitution of the executive department in this particular form were indispensable to the successful action of the government, or attended with advantages sufficient to counterbalance the evils resulting from it, we should, of course, accept the latter with cheerfulness, as the natural price which we must pay for the former; but this does not seem to be the case. The importance attached, in public opinion, to the office of president, is wholly disproportionate to the nature of the political functions connected with it, which are chiefly matters of mere routine.

The constant agitation, which is kept up throughout the country by the struggle for this office, and the great increase of intensity which it gives to party divisions, are, therefore, a clear injury, without any corresponding benefit. If the inconveniences, which we have thus far experienced, be the worst that are likely to result from the existing system, we might endure them with the less reluctance, since, considerable as they in fact are, they are yet trifling, when compared with the terrible oppressions incident to the differently constituted governments of the old world. But there is no small ground for apprehension, that, as the country advances in wealth and population, the inconveniences alluded to may assume a more malignant character than they have hitherto worn. If our institutions are destined, as many suppose, to a premature and violent termination, it can hardly be doubted that the struggle for the presidency will be the immediate occasion of the convulsions by which it will be brought about. Without giving way to gloomy forebodings of contingent, perhaps, on the whole, improbable, results, and assuming that the good sense of the people will be competent to correct, by amendment of the constitution, any error that may become apparent, it is yet certain that, if the unfortunate result alluded to should happen, we shall have sacrificed the solidity and permanence of our government for a bawble of no essential value.

It is somewhat remarkable, that the inconveniences and dangers incident to the nature of elective monarchies, even in their most qualified and limited form, do not seem to have occurred to the minds of the members of the Federal Convention, while deliberating upon this part of the constitution. Their attention was so entirely absorbed by the question of the relative influence of the states in Congress, that they felt comparatively little interest in the executive department, and continued almost mechanically the form in use under the colonial system, without reflecting that the administration of a subject province under the orders of a metropolitan government, and the chief magistracy of an independent state, are functions of an entirely different character, and should be provided for on directly opposite principles. The sagacious mind of Henry, predisposed, as it was, for the reasons above specified, to take an unfavorable view of the plan of the Convention, seized at once upon the weak point in the constitution as the principal object of attack.

The overwhelming power of the president, and its fatal influence upon the independence of the states and the liberty of the people, are the leading topics of his numerous and frequently powerful speeches in the Virginia Convention. There is, doubtless, some, perhaps we may say much, exaggeration in these views; but the experience of half a century has tended, on the whole, to confirm rather than refute them. Of the parties that have subsequently been formed in the country, those which represent most directly the friends of the constitution at the period of the adoption, have not been, by any means, the least conspicuous in denouncing, as a great evil, the undue importance that is attributed, in our system, to the chief executive magistracy. It remains to be seen whether the evil can be cured by the quiet process of amendment, or whether, if it be too deeply implanted in this system to admit of that remedy, it will be kept hereafter, as it has hitherto been, in practical subordination by the sounder and better parts of the system, or will finally assume new degrees of malignity, and exercise upon the whole form of the government the fatal and destructive influence, which the patriotic fears of Henry had led him to anticipate.

It will not be necessary, on the present occasion, to analyze accurately all the speeches made by Henry in the Virginia Convention. They are very numerous, and occupy no inconsiderable portion of the volume of debates. It may be proper, however, to cast a rapid glance over the course of the proceedings, and to indicate, briefly, the part taken by him on the different questions that successively came under discussion.

The Convention met at Richmond, on the 2d of June, 1788. From the great importance of the state of Virginia in the Union, and the care with which the members of the Convention had been selected, it was an assembly hardly less imposing than the Federal Convention itself. Eight states had already ratified the constitution. Five were yet to pass upon it. By the terms of the instrument, the consent of one more would make it binding on the ratifying states. It may well be doubted, however, whether, without the ratification of Virginia, it could have gone into successful operation. Independently of other considerations, Virginia was the residence of

Washington; and there can be no question, that the anticipation of his election as the first president was an essential and indispensable requisite to the practical adoption of the constitution. The proceedings of the Virginia Convention were therefore watched with intense interest throughout the country, and the results of its deliberations looked for with extreme anxiety, both by the friends and enemies of the new system, as decisive on the main question by its ultimate adoption or rejection.

The Convention was organized by the election of Mr. Pendleton as chairman. On the 4th of June, the debate commenced; as a preliminary step, a resolution had been passed that no question should be taken, upon any particular clause in the constitution, before the whole instrument had undergone a full discussion. From the 4th to the 13th of June, the debate was carried on upon the instrument at large. On the 15th, the consideration of the separate clauses began, and it was continued until the 24th. On the 25th, the general discussion was renewed; and, on the 26th, it was closed by the adoption of the constitution. In the debate of the 25th, Henry had proposed a bill of rights and a series of amendments, the adoption of which by the other states was to be made a condition of the ratification of the constitution by Virginia. The proposition, as made by him, was rejected, and the constitution adopted without condition; but, immediately after the vote for the ratification, a committee was raised to report a bill of rights and a series of amendments, to be submitted to the other states in the form prescribed by the constitution. On the 27th, the committee reported the bill of rights and amendments proposed by Henry, and their report was accepted. This proceeding was the last act of the Convention.

The debates in this assembly were more fully and ably reported, than those of any of the other State Conventions, and fill an octavo volume of nearly five hundred closely-printed pages, a volume second only in value, for the student of constitutional law, to the inestimable report of the debates in the Federal Convention by Madison. The discussions of the first thirteen days are particularly interesting. They were managed chiefly by Nicholas, Pendleton, Randolph, Marshall, and Madison, in favor of the adoption, and by Henry, George Mason, Monroe, and Grayson, against it. All these persons were men of the highest order of talent, but the real champions and leaders of the two parties were Henry and Madison. No two men could be more unlike in their intellectual constitution, and each possessed qualities in which he was decidedly superior to the other. Henry excelled his opponent, perhaps, in original power of mind, certainly in brilliancy of imagination, and splendor of natural eloquence. He had also the advantage that belongs to greater experience; the habit of success, and a name endeared to the people by association, with a long career of public service and the highest political and military employments. In calm good sense, instinctive sagacity, extent of information, and clearness of reasoning, he was surpassed by his comparatively youthful rival.

The qualities in which Henry excelled are undoubtedly those that are most likely to produce effect on a popular assembly. It is, therefore, highly creditable to the general intelligence of the Virginia Convention, that they manfully withstood his overwhelming eloquence, backed as it was by the almost irresistible charm attached to his name and character, and yielded their assent to the cool and clear logic of Madison. In accounting for this result, we must doubtless take into view the array of able coadjutors, by whom Madison was supported in the Convention, including even Marshall, who, though he said but little, whenever he did speak, always spoke to the point, with unrivalled power; the example of the other states, where the constitution had already been adopted; and, above all, the general reverence for the character of Washington, who stood behind the curtain as a sort of guardian genius of the precious instrument that bore his signature, unseen, unheard, but exercising a moral power that was deeply felt by every one. But, after making all the necessary allowance for these circumstances, it cannot well be questioned that the influence of Madison, through his talents, character, and persevering exertions, was the immediate cause, in the Virginia Convention, as it had been before in the general one, of the adoption of the constitution. To him belongs the transcendent honor of having first supported, and subsequently sustained and carried through, by means of his own personal influence, at every subsequent stage of its progress, this great charter of our country's prosperity and freedom. We may search in vain the long rolls of history for a higher title to civil and political distinction.

A more particular, though, of course, very cursory, survey of the progress of the debate will show more distinctly how large and important was the part taken in it by the subject of our narrative. After the preliminary proceedings had been terminated, the debate was opened by Henry, who moved for "the reading of the act of Assembly appointing deputies to meet at Annapolis, to consult with those of other states on the situation of the commerce of the United States, the act of Assembly appointing deputies to meet at Philadelphia to revise the articles of confederation, and other public papers relative thereto." The purpose of Henry, in making this motion, was, of course, to introduce the formidable, and certainly not entirely ill-founded objection, that the Federal Convention, in forming a new system, instead of merely revising the old one, had exceeded its powers. The idea was, however, not insisted on, and, after a few remarks by Mr. Pendleton in opposition to it, the motion of Henry was withdrawn. The facility with which this preliminary objection, perhaps the strongest of a positive kind that could be brought against the constitution, was yielded by its most determined and vigorous antagonist, shows already that the moral forces, which were operating indirectly in favor of it, had sapped the strength of opposition even before the debate commenced, and afforded a pregnant indication of the probable issue.

This difficulty having been overcome, the discussion commenced with a speech from Mr. Nicholas, in which he recapitulated, in a forcible manner, and somewhat at large, the principal arguments in favor of the adoption of the plan. He was followed by Henry in a short speech, in which, describing the proposition of the new plan to be, as it really was, a proposition to effect a revolution in the general government, he calls upon its friends to show cause for so extraordinary a proceeding. The country is, to all outward appearance, tranquil and prosperous. In such a state of things, what reasonable motive can be alleged for proceeding to this desperate extremity, which, by general acknowledgment, can only be justified by the existence of misgovernment and oppression in their worst and most intolerable form? In the tenor of this inquiry we find a second evidence of the care with which Henry had surveyed the whole ground, and the skill with which he had selected the positions that he intended successively to occupy. The General Convention had exceeded its powers. This is the first objection, and is in the nature of a plea to the jurisdiction of the court at law. This being waived, a second objection, still preliminary, but of a more substantial character, presents itself. The country is tranquil and prosperous; the people are happy. Under such circumstances, it seems like political insanity to propose an entire revolution in the government.

The friends of the constitution did not meet these objections with any very precise or elaborate reply. They probably deemed it a more politic plan of campaign to reserve their main strength till the positive objections had been stated, rather than to assume the burden of proof, and undertake to show by argument the necessity of a change. Governor Randolph made a short and not very powerful answer to the speech of Henry. He was followed by George Mason, in a speech against the plan, after which Mr. Madison made a very few remarks, which closed the proceedings of the first day of the debates. On the day following, the discussion was continued by Messrs. Pendleton and Lee, in reply to Henry; but it was now apparent, that it was not the intention of the friends of the plan to meet the question upon this ground. Perceiving this, Henry proceeded to unmask his main battery, and occupied the rest of the second day by a long and powerful speech, in which he presented in detail the positive objections. It is, of course, impossible to state them fully in this connection, and the general outline of the argument is familiar to most readers of political history. The leading topics of the speech, as of all those which were made by Henry during the discussion, were the danger of consolidation, and the overwhelming power of the executive.

The speech is badly reported, and in two or three of the most important parts is avowedly imperfect. It probably gives a very inadequate representation of the language of the orator, to say nothing of his looks, tones, and gestures, everything, in short, that is embraced under the significant and comprehensive term *action*. It contains, however, even in the shape in which we have it, many brilliant and powerful passages, one of them containing the celebrated and often quoted phrase, in which the speaker denounces the plan as deformed by "an awful squinting towards monarchy." It is easy to conceive, that, as delivered by the orator himself, it must have produced a prodigious effect upon the assembly.

The system of attack contemplated by the opponents of the plan was now fully developed. They had been compelled by the prudent management of its friends to assume the offensive, and leave to the latter the comparatively easy task of answering positive objections. It was now necessary to take the field in reply, in full force, under the direction of the ablest champions. The two following days, the 6th and 7th of June, were accordingly occupied by long and elaborate speeches from Randolph, Nicholas, Corbin, and Madison, in which they successively surveyed the whole ground taken by Henry, and presented, under every variety of form and color, the most plausible answers that could be made to his objections. At the close of the debate of the 7th, Henry commenced, and continued through the greater part of that of the 8th another long and powerful speech in rejoinder; and was again answered, at great length, on the same and the next following day, by Governor Randolph. After this the discussion was kept up with undaunted spirit, though in a somewhat less regular form, by the principal speakers on both sides, until the 15th, when it was at length brought to a close. The discussion of the separate articles, which occupied the interval between this date and the 23d, was necessarily of a more desultory character, and would not admit of a precise analysis. The debates on the judiciary, which occupied the 20th and 21st, were particularly interesting.

On the 24th, the general discussion was renewed, and Henry now made his final effort, founding his proposition of a ratification on the condition of the acceptance by the other states of a bill of rights and a series of amendments. At the close of this speech, a scene occurred which affords a good example of the manner in which the poetical element has blended itself with the simple truth in the accounts handed down to us of Henry's speeches and life. In the closing passages of his speech, while descanting on the immense importance of the question at issue, Henry appealed to the beings of a superior order, who might be supposed to survey, from their celestial abodes, with deep interest the progress of a struggle involving the future fortunes of half mankind. "To those beings," says Mr. Wirt, on the authority of Judge Archibald Stuart, who was a member of the Convention, and present at the debate, " to those beings he had addressed an invocation with a most thrilling look and action, that made every nerve shudder with supernatural horror, when, lo! a storm at that instant arose, which shook the whole building, and the spirits whom he had called seemed to have come at his bidding. Nor did his eloquence or the storm immediately cease. Availing himself of the incident with a master's art, he seemed to mix in the fight of his ethereal auxiliaries, and, ' rising on the wings of the tempest, to seize upon the artillery of heaven, and direct its fiercest thunders against the heads of his adversaries.' The scene became insupportable, and the House rose without the formality of adjournment, the members rushing from their seats with precipitation and confusion."

The reporter presents the passage in the speech of Henry here alluded to in the following form;

"The honorable gentleman tells you of important blessings, which he imagines will result to us and to mankind in general from the adoption of this system. As for me, I can only see the awful immensity of the dangers with which it is pregnant. I see it. I feel it. I see beings of a higher order anxious concerning our decision. I extend my view beyond the horizon that limits human vision, and behold those superior intelligences anticipating the political revolutions which in process of time may take place in America, and the consequent happiness or misery of mankind. I am led to believe that much of the account on one side or the other will depend on what we now decide. Our own happiness alone is not affected by the event. All nations are interested in the determination. We have it in our own power to secure the happiness of one half of the human race. Its adoption may involve the misery of the other hemisphere."

"Here," says the reporter, in a parenthesis, "a violent storm arose, which put the House in such disorder, that Mr. Henry was obliged to conclude."

Mr. Wirt remarks, in a note, that, "by comparing the statement of Judge Stuart with this passage in the printed debates, the reader may decide how far these may be relied on as specimens of Mr. Henry's eloquence." The passage as reported certainly carries internal evidence of being a very feeble and inadequate transcript of the orator's language; but we suspect that the reporter's parenthesis will be thought by most readers a much more natural and plausible account of the reasons and manner of adjournment, than the glowing statement of the learned judge.

The general discussion was continued on the 25th, and two or three new speakers took, for the first time, a prominent part in the debate; Colonel Innis, then attorney-general of the state, who seems to have been a very remarkable orator, and whose eloquence is characterized by Mr. Wirt, in his usual florid style, as a "splendid conflagration," Judge Tyler, and Zachariah Johnson. Randolph, Henry, Madison, Monroe, and Grayson, mingled, as usual, in the discussion. At the close of this day's debate, the question was taken, and on the two following days the proceedings of the Convention were brought, in the manner that has been already mentioned, to a close.

Although the views of Henry were not adopted by the Convention, he seems to have suffered no diminution of his personal influence in consequence of the part which he took on this occasion. At the session of the Assembly, which was held on the following October, he succeeded in preventing the election of Mr. Madison to the Senate of the United States, and in carrying that of Richard Henry Lee and Mr. Grayson, the latter of whom had been in the Convention an active opponent of the constitution. At the same session, he moved a resolution requesting Congress to call another General Convention, for the purpose of amending the instrument as adopted. A motion was made to amend this resolution by substituting another, inviting Congress to propose to the states, in the constitutional way, the bill of rights and series of amendments proposed by Henry, and adopted at the Richmond Convention. This motion was rejected, and the original proposal of Henry was adopted by a triumphant majority of more than two to one.

Thus terminated the action of Henry upon the great reform effected in the government by the adoption of the federal constitution. While we render the fullest justice to the correctness of his intentions, and to the superiority of talent and eloquence with which he supported his views in the Convention, we may pronounce it, without hesitation, a most fortunate thing for the country that they did not prevail. Still more fortunate will it be, if the dangers which he apprehended shall prove, in the sequel, to have been imaginary, and not to have been adjourned for a time, only to burst upon us with greater fury in proportion to the immense augmentation, which will have taken place in the interval in the extent and population of the country. The enemies of liberal constitutions abroad generally look forward to the early occurrence among us of some such catastrophe, and are sustained in their gloomy forebodings by the opinions of many of our most judicious and best informed citizens. Yet when we find the superior liberality of our institutions, accompanied, as it thus far has been, by a corresponding superiority in the intelligence, morality, and general well-being of the people, we may venture, perhaps, to regard such apprehensions as groundless, and to consider the establishment of our republican empire as the opening of a new and more auspicious chapter in the history of man.

CHAPTER VIII.

Retirement of Henry from political and professional Life. — Domestic Occupations. — Death and Character.

The proceedings detailed in the preceding chapter were the last, of a political character, in which Henry was engaged. It is understood, that, on the retirement of Mr. Jefferson from the office of Secretary of State, Henry was requested to take charge of that department of the government; and it is rumored, that, at a later period, during the administration of John Adams, he was offered successively the appointments of Minister to France and to Spain. At the close of the year 1796, he was elected by the legislature Governor of the commonwealth, but declined the office.

He seems to have taken no very decided part in the political controversies that grew up after the adoption of the federal constitution, but favored alternately the views of one or the other party, according to his own private opinion of the merits of the particular question upon which they were for the time divided. He disapproved Mr. Jay's treaty with Great Britain; but, after it had been ratified by the Senate, and become constitutionally the law of the land, he deemed it the duty of every citizen to concur in carrying it into effect in his appropriate sphere of action, whether political or personal, and condemned the course of those members of the House of Representatives of the United States, who endeavored to prevent the appropriation necessary for this purpose. He also publicly expressed his approbation of the Alien and Sedition Laws, and his disapprobation of the celebrated Kentucky and Virginia resolutions. So strong was his apprehension of danger to the public tranquillity, from the policy which dictated these resolutions, that it induced him to break the determination, which he had previously formed, to take no further part in the public affairs; and, in the spring of the year 1799, he presented himself to the electors of Charlotte county, in which he resided, as a candidate for the State Assembly.

Although his avowed object, in seeking an election, was to oppose the views of a party which predominated throughout the State, his personal influence was so great that he was elected by his usual commanding majority. After his election was known, it was deemed by the republican leaders a matter of so much importance, that great exertions were made to bring into the Assembly their most distinguished advocates, for the purpose of neutralizing his influence. Giles, Taylor of Caroline, Nicholas, and a number of younger men, conspicuous for talent and eloquence, were deputed to the Assembly. Madison himself retired from Congress, and accepted a place in the Virginia legislature for the purpose of encountering the great champion on his own ground. Had Henry taken his seat, it would have been a singular spectacle to see these distinguished men leading on, as before, their respective parties, but each, so far as party connections were concerned, occupying a position directly opposite to that which he had held in the State Convention. The republican party had a large majority in the Assembly, and it is altogether probable that Henry would have found it as difficult to stem the torrent of public opinion on this occasion, as he had on the preceding one; but the point was never brought to a practical issue. A disease, under which he had been suffering for two years, came to a crisis about the time of his election to the Assembly, and terminated fatally on the 6th of June, 1799.

At the new session of the Assembly, a member of the federal party moved the following resolution;

"The General Assembly of Virginia, as a testimonial of their veneration for the character of their late illustrious fellow-citizen, Patrick Henry, whose unrivalled eloquence and superior talents were, in times of peculiar peril and distress, so uniformly, so powerfully and successfully devoted to the cause of freedom and of his country; and, in order to incite the present and future generations to an imitation of his virtues, and an emulation of his fame;

"Resolve, That the Executive be authorized and requested to procure a marble bust of the said Patrick Henry, at the public expense, and to cause the same to be placed in one of the niches of the hall of the House of Delegates."

The reception, which this motion met with in the Assembly, affords a striking proof how completely, at periods of high party excitement, a difference of opinion on the current questions of the day is permitted to outweigh every consideration of a more general character. The mover of the resolution, as well as the illustrious subject of it, was regarded by the majority, not merely as an opponent, but as an apostate; and, although every member would have doubtless concurred in the view taken of Henry's general character, and in the propriety of the measure recommended, the action on the resolutions was determined by a strictly party vote. A member of the majority moved to lay it on the table. The member who offered it replied, with warmth, that, if it were so disposed of, he would never call it up again. The motion to lay on the table prevailed, and the resolution was, in consequence, never acted on.

The charge of apostasy is habitually made, in this and other countries, against all who take a course, in political or religious affairs, different from that pursued by a party with which they have habitually acted, and is generally intended to intimate a suspicion of corrupt or interested motives. In reality, a difference of this kind does not, in all cases, suppose even inconsistency in principle. The questions upon which parties are divided are continually changing; and, with the few who form opinions for themselves, it must be a matter of mere accident whether, in reasoning upon a new state of things, they come to the same conclusions, which are drawn by others, with whom they had agreed before upon a different subject.

In the present case, it might, perhaps, have appeared more natural that Henry, who had opposed the federal constitution, as tending too strongly to concentrate power in the government, should have afterwards favored the strictest construction of that instrument; while, on the other hand, it may be thought singular that Madison, the great champion of a vigorous general government in the Federal and Virginia Conventions, should have insisted on the construction more favorable to state rights and individual liberty. But, after all, the questions of the Alien and Sedition Laws, and of our relations with France, which formed the principal topics of party controversy at this period, were essentially different from that of the adoption or rejection of the federal constitution; and it is quite unnecessary, and of course uncharitable and unjust, to suppose that either of the two great Virginia statesmen was governed, in the course he pursued, by any other than the purest and most patriotic motives.

This is now universally acknowledged in the case of Mr. Madison, whose name and memory are equally respected by all parties; and it is presumed, that the verdict of public opinion is not less favorable in regard to Henry. In neither case could there be the slightest pretence for the imputation of interested views; and both, in taking a course which necessarily exposed them to a good deal of temporary obloquy, evinced a moral courage in a high degree honorable to their general characters. In a letter to his daughter, Mrs. Aylett, written in 1796, Henry repels the idea of any change in his opinions, upon the leading principles of political philosophy, and gives his reasons, founded on the merits of the particular cases, for differing from his former associates upon the points then at issue. It is unnecessary, for the present purpose, to pursue the subject in any further detail.

After his retirement from political life, Henry continued for several years the practice of his laborious profession with undiminished reputation and success. In the class of cases which require or admit the dignity of eloquence, he stood, by general acknowledgment, at the head of the bar, and though less familiar with the technical learning of the law than some others, yet, whenever the questions involved were of sufficient interest to engage his attention, he qualified himself for the occasion, and maintained his usual undisputed preëminence. The celebrated case of the British debts, which he argued twice for two or three days in succession, was, perhaps, the most important in which he was engaged. A report of his second argument is given, at great length, by Mr. Wirt, from the notes of Robertson, the reporter of the debates in the Virginia Convention; and although, doubtless, (as every such report must necessarily be,) a very imperfect copy of the orator's language, conveys the impression of the highest order of forensic ability. In 1794, he finally retired from professional life, and, with the exception of the brief periods of political action already alluded to, passed his remaining years in the bosom of his family.

The steady pursuit of his profession, to which he had of late devoted himself, had supplied him with a competent fortune. By his two marriages he was the father of fifteen children, eleven of whom, with his second wife, were living at his death. He thus enjoyed the highest satisfaction that can belong to the declining period of life, in the society and affection of a numerous offspring. He retained, to the last, the cheerful and sportive temperament which formed, in youth, his most remarkable characteristic. He was frequently found by his visiters joining in the games of his little grandchildren, and entrancing them with the music of the same violin, which had so often in his early days seduced him from the graver occupations of the counting-room. His love of conversation and society had always been intense;

and, being now relieved from care and business of every kind, he gave himself up without restraint to this cherished passion. He was always surrounded by a circle of family connections and neighbors, including a constant succession of strangers from other states and foreign countries, who were attracted, by his high reputation, to visit him at his residence. In the court before his door there was a large walnut-tree, under which he often passed his summer evenings and entertained his friends.

Imagination can present no brighter picture of a happy old age, than is exhibited in the real life of Henry; and, when we compare this charming spectacle with that of the cares and privations which have clouded the closing years of some of our greatest revolutionary patriots, we are forced to acknowledge, that the strict private economy with which Henry has sometimes been reproached as a fault, when combined, as it was in his case, with a genial temperament and a liberal discharge of all the duties of life, was not so much a venial error as an actual, positive, and most important virtue. He had been always strongly impressed with the importance of religion, and had studied with care the best books on the subject that came within his reach. In the year 1790, he published, at his own expense, for gratuitous distribution among the people, an edition of Soame Jenyns's View of the Internal Evidences of Christianity. Among his favorite works were Doddridge's Rise and Progress of Religion in the Soul, and Butler's Analogy of Religion, Natural and Revealed; a selection not less honorable to his literary taste, than to his religious character. In his last days, he dwelt with augmented interest on these great subjects.

To a friend, who visited him not long before his death, and found him engaged in reading the Bible, he remarked, "This is a book worth more than all the others that were ever printed. It is my misfortune not to have found time to read it with the proper attention and feeling till lately. I trust in the mercy of Heaven, that it is not yet too late." It appears, from the language used on this occasion, and from other circumstances, that he inclined to what is popularly called the Orthodox view of Christianity; but he was entirely free from sectarian dogmatism, and did not even connect himself in form with any denomination of Christians. He had probably reached, by the power of his own instinctive sagacity, that higher view towards which the public mind is now struggling, without having yet fully attained it, which regards the points that divide the different sects from each other as comparatively immaterial, and the essence of religion as residing in those that are common to them all.

In his person, Henry was tall and thin, with a
slight stoop of the shoulders. His complexion
was dark, and his face furrowed by deep lines of
care and thought, which gave it a somewhat
severe aspect. In his youth, he was rather in-
attentive to his dress; but in his later years,
especially on public occasions, and while he occupied the executive chair, he paid, in this respect,
a proper regard to the decorum required by his
position in society. At the bar of the General
Assembly he always appeared in a full suit of
black cloth, or velvet, with a tie-wig dressed and
powdered in the highest style of forensic fashion;
and in the winter season he wore over his other
apparel, in accordance with the usage of the
time, an ample scarlet cloak. As he advanced
in years, he also exchanged the rusticity of his
youthful manners for a deportment distinguished
by entire self-possession, and, on proper occasions,
by an air of stateliness and elegance. He is
represented, by those who have been present
when he has entered the hall of the Assembly for
the purpose of arguing some important case, as
"saluting the House all round with a dignity, and
even majesty, that would have done honor to the
most polished courtier in Europe."

The leading traits in his intellectual and moral
character have been often alluded to in the
course of this narrative, and are shown too clearly

in his practical life to require an elaborate recapitulation. He possessed an instinctive sagacity, which supplied, to a great extent, the deficiencies of his education; a moral courage, which led him to spurn at all considerations of mere temporary expediency, when he was once satisfied where the right lay, and a naturally noble and generous heart. To these latter qualities he owed his extraordinary efficiency and success as a public speaker. Eloquence, no doubt, supposes, in general, the natural gift of an easy, copious, and flowing utterance; but this is not a rare endowment, and, when wholly or chiefly relied upon for effect, is apt to tire, rather than convince or delight an audience. It rises into eloquence only when it becomes the expression of powerful thought, and especially deep feeling.

While the speaker only gratifies the ear with melodious tones, and pleases the eye with graceful gestures, he is in some degree successful, but does not produce the highest possible effect. Nor does he reach the perfection of his art, when he merely succeeds in convincing the judgment by a train of sound or plausible reasoning. It is only when he acts upon the moral part of our nature, by stirring and successful appeals to the passions, that he kindles enthusiasm, and becomes for the moment a sort of divinity. The power of producing such effects, of making such appeals with success, is itself, in a great measure, the result of a naturally keen sensibility, which is accordingly represented by the greatest critic of antiquity as the foundation of excellence in public speaking. *Pectus est quod facit disertum.* But even this essential requisite is not sufficient; for the orator must not only move and melt, but, on proper occasions, alarm, terrify, and subjugate his hearers. In order to succeed in this, he must possess the moral courage, the undaunted self-possession, the overwhelming energy of character, which enables him to point the artillery of his eloquence at its object, under all circumstances, and without regard to personal consequences.

In the possession, in a much higher degree than others, of these transcendent moral qualifications for success in oratory, lay the secret of the supremacy of Henry over his distinguished contemporaries and rivals, some of whom, as, for instance, Richard Henry Lee, were much above him in literary accomplishments and external graces of manner. In this lay the peculiar *charm*, which, by general acknowledgment, hung upon his lips, as it does upon those of every truly eloquent speaker, and which the hearer can only feel without being able to describe. Description, in fact, embraces only such particulars as meet the eye and ear; but the sympathy, which rouses and inflames the moral part of our nature, is a kind of magnetic impulse, that passes from the heart of the speaker to that of his audience, eluding observation, and only recognized in its overwhelming results.

The language, which forms the medium for the transmission of this impulse, and which is identical in its essence with the highest poetry, transcends, of course, the talent of the ordinary reporter. It can never be reduced to a permanent form, excepting when the orator himself combines with the requisites of his own art the talent of a first-rate writer. To this rare combination of powers we owe the finished specimens, which have come down to us, of the eloquence of the two great orators of Greece and Rome. Chatham, the first of British speakers, either wanted the talent of writing, or did not exercise it in his own speeches; which correspond very imperfectly with the effects, that we know to have attended their delivery. Henry, like him, had never cultivated, and rarely exercised, the art of writing; the reports of his speeches, while they furnish an outline of the argument, convey no image of the glowing language in which it was clothed, still less of the moral inspiration that chiefly gave it effect. They fall, of course, far below his fame; and it is, after all, on the faith of mere tradition, attested, however, by facts too numerous and of too public a character to leave it in any way doubtful, that the present and future generations will acknowledge the justice of his claim to the proud title, that has been given him, of the greatest orator of the New World.

NOTE,

BY THE EDITOR.

Virginia Resolutions on the Stamp Act.

[See p. 266.]

A copy of these Resolutions was sent to the Ministry by Governor Fauquier. The following is an extract from his letter to the Lords of Trade, dated Williamsburg, June 5th, 1765.

"On Saturday, the 1st instant, I dissolved the Assembly, after passing all the bills, except one, which were ready for my assent. The four Resolutions, which I have now the honor to enclose to your Lordships, will show your Lordships the reason of my conduct, and, I hope, justify it. I will relate the whole proceeding to your Lordships in as concise a manner as I am able.

"On Wednesday, the 29th of May, just at the end of the session, when most of the members had left the town, there being but thirty-nine present, of one hundred and sixteen, of which the House of Burgesses now consists, a motion was made to take into consideration the Stamp Act, a copy of which had crept into the House; and in a committee of the whole House five resolutions were proposed and agreed to, all by very small majorities. On Thursday, the 30th, they were reported and agreed to by the House, the number being as before in the committee; the greatest majority being twenty-two to seventeen; for the fifth resolution, twenty to nineteen only. On Friday, the 31st, there having happened a small alteration in the House, there was an attempt to strike all the Resolutions off the Journals. The fifth, which was thought the most offensive, was accordingly struck off; but it did not succeed as to the other four. I am informed the gentlemen had two more resolutions in their pocket, but finding the difficulty they had in carrying the fifth, which was by a single voice, and knowing them to be more virulent and inflammatory, they did not produce them.

"The most strenuous opposers of this rash heat were the late Speaker, the King's Attorney, and Mr. Wythe; but they were overpowered by the young, hot, and giddy members. In the course of the debates, I have heard that very indecent language was used by a Mr. Henry, a young lawyer, who had not been above a month a member of the House, and who carried all the young members with him. So that I hope I am authorized at least in saying, that there is cause to doubt, whether this would have been the sense of the colony, if most of their representatives had done their duty by attending to the end of the session."

Shortly after this letter arrived in London, the Rockingham ministry came into power, and Mr. Secretary Conway wrote a mild and conciliatory reply, dated St. James's, September 14th.

"It is with great pleasure," he says, "I received his Majesty's commands to declare to you his gracious approbation of your conduct. His Majesty and his servants are satisfied, that the precipitate Resolutions you sent home did not take their rise from any remissness or inattention in you; nor is his Majesty at all inclined to suppose, that any instance of diffidence or dissatisfaction could be founded in the general inclination of his ancient and loyal colony of Virginia. The nature of the thing, and your representations, induce a persuasion that those ill-advised Resolutions owed their birth to the violence of some individuals, who, taking advantage of a thin Assembly, so far prevailed as to publish their own unformed opinions to the world as the sentiments of the colony.

"But his Majesty will not, by the prevalence of a few men at a certain moment, be persuaded to change the opinion or lessen the confidence he has always entertained of the colony of Virginia, which has always experienced the protection of the crown. His Majesty's servants, therefore, with entire reliance on your prudence, and on the virtue and wisdom of the colony intrusted to your care, persuade themselves, that, when a full Assembly shall calmly and maturely deliberate on these Resolutions, they will see and be themselves alarmed at the dangerous tendency and mischievous consequences, which they might be productive of, both to the mother country and to the colonies, which are the equal objects of his Majesty's parental care, and whose mutual happiness and prosperity certainly require a confidential reliance of the colonies upon the mother country."

The above extracts explain the proceedings of the Assembly in passing the Resolutions, and the manner in which the British government thought proper to view them at the time.

A shade of mystery hangs over these Resolutions. All the accounts agree, that, when they went out to the world, they produced a very great excitement in the public mind, and had an extraordinary influence in prompting the subsequent movements. But when we now read them, as recorded by the pen of Mr. Henry himself, even including the fifth resolution, which was rejected by the Assembly, it is impossible to discover in what their exciting tendency consisted. The same sentiments, clothed in language as strong, had before been expressed by other assemblies and public bodies. Mr. Wirt has shown, from the printed Journals, that the first four Resolutions only were passed by the Virginia Assembly, and that the last two of these were considerably modified by amendments. Now, these four Resolutions, whether in their original or amended form, manly and bold as they are, contain nothing more than a declaration of sentiments, which had already been declared and published by other Assemblies.

The fifth resolution, which passed at first by a majority of one vote, and which, upon a reconsideration, was expunged from the Journals, is as follows;

"Resolved, therefore, That the General Assembly of this colony have the sole right and power to lay taxes and impositions upon the inhabitants of this colony; and that every attempt to vest such power in any person or persons whatsoever, other than the General Assembly aforesaid, has a manifest tendency to destroy British as well as American freedom."

If this resolution speaks in more pointed language than the others, it does not assume a higher tone than was manifested in the proceedings of some of the Assemblies the year before. The Massachusetts Assembly say, June 13th, 1764, in a letter to their agent in London, which was to be communicated to the Ministry, "The silence of the province should have been imputed to any cause, even to despair, rather than be construed into a tacit cession of their rights, or an acknowledgment of a right in the Parliament of Great Britain to impose duties and taxes upon a people, who are not represented in the House of Commons." And the New York Assembly, in their petition to the House of Commons in October of the same year, after claiming a freedom from Parliamentary taxation, " proceed to inform the Commons of Great Britain, that the people of this colony, inspired by the genius of their mother country, nobly disdain the thought of claiming that exemption as a privilege. They found it on a basis more honorable, solid, and stable; they challenge it, and glory in it, as their right." The letter and petition, from which these extracts are taken, were published. Other declarations, of a similar character, might be cited. What is there, even in Mr. Henry's fifth resolution, that shows a more determined spirit, or that was more likely to touch the popular feeling?

It is certain, nevertheless, that the Virginia Resolutions, as they came before the public, did produce a great excitement, and contributed in a remarkable degree to rouse the spirit of the people throughout the colonies. Governor Bernard says, in writing to the ministry from Boston, August 15th, 1765, "Two or three months ago I thought that this people would submit to the Stamp Act. Murmurs were indeed continually heard, but they seemed to be such as would die away. But the publishing of the Virginia Resolves proved an alarm-bell to the disaffected." And Hutchinson says, "These resolves were expressed in such terms, that many people, upon the first surprise, pronounced them treasonable." (Hist. of Massachusetts, Vol. III. p. 119.) Such an impression could not have been produced by Mr. Henry's five resolutions, as reported by himself, and much less so by the four actually adopted by the Assembly.

We must look farther, therefore, for an explanation. It would seem, that a spurious copy of these Resolves was first circulated in the newspapers, and afterwards printed in the "Prior Documents," Gordon's History of the Revolution, Ramsay's History, and Marshall's Life of Washington. In this copy, the third resolution, as passed by the Virginia Assembly, is wholly omitted; the fifth reported by Mr. Henry is essentially altered from his draft; and two additional ones are appended, of which no mention is made in Mr. Henry's remarks on the subject. They are as follow;

"Resolved, That his Majesty's liege people, the inhabitants of this colony, are not bound to yield obedience to any law or ordinance whatsoever, designed to impose any taxation whatsoever upon them, other than the laws or ordinances of the General Assembly aforesaid.

"Resolved, That any person who shall, by speaking or writing, assert or maintain, that any person or persons, other than the General Assembly of this colony, have any right or power to impose or lay any taxation whatsoever on the people here, shall be deemed an enemy to his Majesty's colony."

Gordon represents these two resolves as having been read in the Assembly. In the "Prior Documents" it is stated, that "they were not passed, but only drawn up by the committee." They are doubtless the same alluded to by Governor Fauquier, as the two which "the gentlemen had in their pocket," but which they did not produce, on account of the ill success of the fifth, "knowing them to be more virulent and inflammatory." There is no evidence that they were written by Henry, or even that he had seen them. Yet these two Resolutions were sent abroad, not only as his composition, but as among those which had been adopted by the Virginia Assembly. This latter circumstance gave them a currency, and a weight, which produced the powerful influence on the public mind described by the writers of that period. The newspapers soon took up the vindication and defence of the Virginia Resolves. "The spirit discovered in them," says Hutchinson, "was applauded as worthy of imitation, and the declaration in them, that *all who maintained the right of Parliament should be deemed enemies to the colo-*

ny, had a tendency to bring on those acts of violence, which soon after were committed in Boston." Hutchinson here obviously speaks of the last resolution, and apparently without knowing that ^id not proceed from the Virginia Assembly.

We are hence led to the inference, that a spurious copy of the Virginia Resolves was at first put in circulation; that these were so well suited to the spirit of the time, that no attempts were made to correct the error; that three of these only were drafted and proposed by Patrick Henry; and that the two, which had emanated from a private and uncertain source, were chiefly instrumental in producing the marvellous effects so universally ascribed to them, and this because it was supposed they had been adopted by the Virginia Assembly, or at least approved by the distinguished patriots of the Old Dominion, which, as standing in the first rank among the colonies, justly exercised a commanding influence

www.ingramcontent.com/pod-product-compliance
Lightning Source LLC
Chambersburg PA
CBHW050801160426
43192CB00010B/1601